DEDICATION

Dad, you taught me to be a great man, husband, and father. You instilled in me curiosity, responsibility, adventure, and love. You encouraged me to follow my passions and dreams. May this book reveal the brilliant harvest of the seeds of excellence you've sown since I was a child. I love you, Daddio. Thank you.

This book was designed to read one of two ways:

1) Read through to the end like a novel. Enjoy it. Go to www.LegacyCodeBook.com/yourlegacy where I'll personally walk you through the exercises.

2) Have a pen and a journal with you as you read through. Circle, underline, highlight, make notes in the book and do the exercises right then in your journal. After you are done go to www.LegacyCodeBook.com/yourlegacy and go over them again.

Do this and this book will be an asset in your life and in creating the legacy you desire.

Enjoy,

Table of Contents

FOREWORD

"Why Should I Read ANOTHER Self-Help Book?"

That's probably what you're asking yourself right now, to be honest; it's a fair question.

A VERY fair question!

With so many books on self-development, success, and happiness already in print, it may seem that pretty much anything and everything that could be said about these subjects has been said already and, in some ways that would be true.

After all, very little of what finds its way onto our bookshelves (or eBook readers!) is of the uniquely original variety and, instead, tends to be the general rehash of ideas that that most of us have already become VERY familiar with. One could arguably put forward the case that yet ANOTHER book on these topics adds very little to the genre or the people who seek out answers within it.

Yet there's also another case that could be made and that, with your permission, I'd like to make regarding the book you now hold in your hands; it's that whilst the general INFORMATION across any given genre may tend to stem from the same sources and share the same general message, it's not always the information itself that contains the REAL value to the reader.

Especially in this day and age when one can visit the "university of Google" from any mobile device and find "the facts" and information within seconds at the mere touch of a button.

In fact, you could say that the fact that there's so MUCH information out there right now is the very REASON that people are struggling or, as I like to say, "People are drowning in information and yet thirsting for knowledge."

If that sounds like you, like you're one of those who are drowning in information and who constantly finds yourself saying "I know WHAT to do, I just can't seem to get myself to do it!" and that you know full well that you don't need more "dressed up" information about success and happiness in your life but rather, what you need is a means to translate information into IMPLEMENTATION then I'm sure that you'll love what my good friend Armando Cruz is about to share with you within the pages of this book.

You see, as smart and intellectual a guy Armando is (and he's VERY smart!), his ability to read, understand and memorize what he studies is not (what I would term) his source of Majik; those gifts and attributes we each possess that make the difficult seem easy, the daunting seem exciting and the confusing seem clear. Armando's Majik is a unique and inspiring blend

8

of creativity, productivity and community. Armando is that rare blend of individual who uses his creativity to not only dream of what his life could be but blends that with action-taking productivity to bring those dreams to life (even in small ways) and then generously and open-heartedly shares both the experiences and the results they provide with others so that they can do the same.

In every way that counts, Armando is a MASTER implementer who has learned to take action on every area of his life in ways that most could only dream of, earning a masters degree in physical therapy, starting a successful therapy and personal training practice, becoming an accomplished speaker, writer, blogger and ultra-distance marathon runner to name but a few of his professional accomplishments and, perhaps more impressively, learning to take action on the things in life that REALLY matter and that lead to having more love, more light and more laughter in our lives.

Whether it be camping with his children, designing and making tools and knives or carving a gift in his workshop to cheer up a friend in need, making a windsail to 'surf' a hurricane or the seemingly ubiquitous creation of birthday watermelon carvings for kids, Armando has a wonderful and child-like way of approaching creativity and combining it with a deep and decidedly adult way of both taking action and finding the best ways to gift the results to others.

And, in every way that counts, that's what *The Legacy Code* is REALLY about.

It's about learning how to act upon and implement those things that make the REAL difference to how we feel about ourselves and our experiences and we live out the days of our lives.

Within the pages of this book Armando does a wonderful job of sharing not just the concepts and ideas but the practical, roll-up-your-sleeves-

and-take-action processes and practices that make the REAL difference.

As you'll soon come to learn, Armando believes that in very real terms, each and every one of us can become R.I.C.H and experience life more powerfully, more enjoyably and more beautifully than most of us have come to believe is possible for us.

Fortunately for you, within this very book, he's willing to tell you how.

I invite you to not only read the words but also to engage fully in what you're about to learn from Armando and to, perhaps for the first time, make creating and implementation your greatest priority.

Become one of the few who says, "I know what to do AND I'm doing it!" Because, after all, what better way is there to create your legacy than through taking action, right?

- Dax Moy

Author of *The MAGIC Hundred,* Founder Of The GuRu Project, Creator Of The MindMAP Coaching Institute

INTRODUCTION

"What's the hardest area you've had issues with balancing in your life?" I asked my dad. He replied, "Family". My jaw dropped. The man that I look up to, the man who taught me how to be an honorable man, a growth-minded husband and an adventurous father just told me he wished he'd spent more time with the family. The reason this shocked me was because growing up, I was blown away at all the time he had spent with us. I never saw any of my friends' dads spend that amount of time with them. I used the way he prioritized the family as the template for how I wanted to be with my family.

We are going to dive deeper about this soon but first let me introduce myself. My name is Armando Cruz. I am a husband, father, legacy coach, lifestyle physical therapist, adventurer, ultra-marathoner, and connoisseur of experiences. I love challenging myself with grueling physical tests of endurance and grit to help me grow as a man, husband, father, and creator. I've scaled mountains and run through deserts, and swamps. I've surfed hurricanes and climbed rock slabs in the moonlight. Some of my most memorable adventures, however, have come through fatherhood, like the time I went camping with my 8-year-old son in a snake and alligator-infested swamp. My son still talks about the awesome time we had!

For the past 14 years, I have been helping men, women, and families optimize their health, mindset, vision, and legacy through my company Cruz Country Fitness & Physical Therapy. I've helped entrepreneurs, CEOs, law enforcement officers, military personnel, and professional athletes. Each of my clients varied in his or her goals but each one of them had a greater interest in thriving and operating from excellence rather than just surviving.

The reason I decided to write this book is that I have specifically spent the past four years coaching entrepreneurial married men in helping them create more powerful legacies. I have coached each man in showing up more powerfully in his health, his business, his family, and his marriage and to better understand and enlarge the impact he is creating in his community and the world at large. One of the themes that surfaced over and over, and over again, when working with my clients, working in men's groups, and being a part of masterminds, is the sacrifice we men make to attain financial success. Oftentimes, this success comes at the expense of our health and/or our marriage and/or our families. Can you relate?

I recall speaking with one of my clients on the steps of his house overlooking his pool. He started out as an electrician, worked his way up the ranks of the company he worked for, eventually bought the company and grew it to one of the biggest local electrical companies. I remember him saying, "I have more money than ever before and yet, I rarely get to see my wife and kids. Every day feels like Groundhog Day. I wake up early, shower, and go to work. The day is a blur and then I end up in the shower again at night and wonder where did the day go?" He was a financially successful businessman and yet he was broke in the other areas of his life.

Many men are uncertain of themselves, of their future, and in the reasons why they make the decisions they make. They experience a feeling of loss of identity and purpose. Many men who are financially successful find themselves asking, "Is that all there is?" "What's the next thing that I can achieve?"

Many of my clients expressed, "I feel like I'm chasing a rainbow. No matter how far I go the rainbow just moves further away." Perhaps you can relate? Have you ever worked hard to achieve something only to find when you got there you couldn't appreciate it because you wanted something else? I know I've been there and so have many of my clients.

Many men lacked a positive and consistent father figure or male role model in their lives, who could have clarified what being a man meant. I am blessed to have had both an amazing father and mother. I believe that having confident, loving, supportive parents truly has positively shaped who I am and how I want to serve in this world. They gave me the template for the kind of husband and father I want to be for my family. They taught me the power of having passion and intent to contribute and serve at a greater capacity.

My goal was to write a book that would give you clarity about who you are today, who you want to become, and provide you with a guide to help you construct your living legacy. I want to provide you with a mirror so you can reflect on your current legacy. I also want to give you a framework of how to define and create your legacy in a way that will inspire and excite you.

I wrote this book to serve men like you and your family on a grander scale. Part of the legacy I want to create is to help men show up more powerfully and authentically in their lives. This is important because I believe if men show up more powerfully and authentically we will have more fulfilled marriages, which make for unified families, and which in turn build productive, connected, and thriving communities.

The past four years I've been coaching growth minded men on how to purposely and powerfully create their legacy. I believe understanding different perspectives is important to creating a clearer more powerful message. In addition to the years of coaching, the mentors I had, and the experiences I've had, I also interviewed 111 men to get their perspectives.

Here are a few of the patterns that kept coming up when I was interviewing these men:

- The top three areas that men felt they needed to improve in were health, family, and leadership.
- The men that were practicing and involved in their faith, meaning that they read scripture and attend church regularly all expressed a grander vision of legacy. They felt that legacy was about fulfilling God's purpose for them.
- Fathers thought about legacy more often than single men.
- The two biggest obstacles that men perceived as preventing them from reaching their goals were fear and uncertainty.

BEFORE WE CONTINUE...

Who is this book **not** for?

This book is not for the man who is unconcerned about his existence. It's not for the man who thinks everything in his life is perfect. It's not for

19

the man who is not willing to question everything he has. It's not for the man that has no desire to grow or to provide more value and excellence in his life, his family's lives, and in his community. This book is not for men who just want the status quo, or who want to get by as an average individual. My guess is if you are reading this, you are not that guy.

Who **is** this book for?

This book is for men who want to grow. This is for men who want to create a legacy that inspires them, one they will get to experience while they are alive. This is for men who want to live out their legacy daily so that there will be no doubt that it is the legacy they leave behind. This is for men who reject complacency. This is for men who are not content with where they are because they know there is a deeper potential itching to come out. This is also for the woman who wants to understand her man better. (While this book is written for men, the principles taught in this book can just as powerfully and positively impact the lives of women and their legacies as well.)

Are you this man?

YES!!!

Then it's time to go on an adventure!

To best guide you, I have divided The Legacy Code into 5 sections: Awareness, Vision, Purpose, Process, and Implementation.

Section 1 is Awareness. In this section I will guide you in discovering what legacy is, what you want your legacy to be, how to align with your legacy, and how to identify the pitfalls.

Section 2 is Vision. In this section, you will explore what your vision is of your legacy. It is the "What" of your legacy, meaning what people say, the experiences that you leave, the impact that you have, essentially what you created, connected, contributed, and lived out.

Section 3 is Purpose. This section is a step commonly skipped over but it is vital to complete because it is where you will gain clarity about why you have the vision of your legacy. When you discover your purpose or your why, you will have that magnet that pulls you towards your legacy. When you understand purpose, life doesn't get in your way, rather, it amplifies your path.

Section 4 is Process. Your Process (a.k.a. plan of attack) is how you will live out and create your legacy. In this section, you will discover how to craft the plan to make the vision of your legacy a reality.

Section 5 is Implementation. Implementation is the doing of the work, the execution of the plan. When you do the work, your actions do the talking. In this section, you will combine your awareness, vision, purpose, and process and breathe life into it by putting it into action. You will execute your process by setting up the daily actions to create the legacy you want to live.

What can you expect to get out of this book?

You can expect to get out of this book what you put into it. It may seem odd to say, but in all honesty, this isn't a magic pill.

What this book will do, is give you an opportunity to gain more clarity, more direction, more support and more focus as you purposely live out your legacy day in and day out. As you craft it, create it, and build it, with your actions.

Henry David Thoreau said, "The mass of men lead quiet lives of desperation." Meaning, most men live a life they wish would be better but just keep doing what they've been doing and continue to grind away at a life of obscurity and lacking fulfillment.

If you are the type of man who likes to create and doesn't like to leave things to chance; if you want to be proactive, this book will provide a blueprint. It will give you a path. It's not the only way to carve out your legacy, but based on neuroscience, psychology, experience, and passion. I can tell you that if you are looking for a way to escape obscurity and live a life unleashed where you feel you are living your life fulfilled, inspired, and on purpose, then this is the book for you.

If you are the type of man who likes more interaction than a book, I've created a special course that will walk you through the legacy creation process. I created this course just for you since you've made the decision to invest in yourself by reading this book. Visit to access this course absolutely FREE. www.LegacyCodeBook.com/yourlegacy

A LOOK INSIDE

Why am I doing this?

My fascination with legacy began because of how much I looked up to my dad and the example he set as a husband and father. I wanted my kids to experience the amazing upbringing that my parents gave me. The bond I have with my father is one I work daily to cultivate with my kids, where I can teach them by example.

My father is a civil engineer, carpenter, general contractor, and inventor. He always made things. He made the first running stroller before there were running strollers. He made it out of wood, metal, and wagon wheels. We called it "El Carreton" which means, "the wagon" in Spanish. My mother, my three siblings and I would ride in El Carreton along with our cooler, toys, and beach chairs while my father would run pushing us to the beach that was almost seven miles away. My father approached everything he made and did to make it last a lifetime. For me, that's the kind of legacy I want to build.

Picture Credit: Author

31 years after my father built "El Carreton," the original jog stroller, I get to use it with my kids. My wife, my two oldest kids, and I are out for a fun, family run in the park.

I remember going to the theater to watch the 1993 movie *Airborne*. It featured extreme inline skating. I saw guys doing flips and twists on a half-pipe ramp. I was blown away and wanted to do the same. After the movie, my father and I talked about making a ramp. Then during the winter break my dad, cousin, and I actually made an 8-foot half-pipe ramp in my backyard.

My dad had a way of creating opportunities to spend quality time with me, to teach me principles that I could live by, and practical skills I could always use. Through this project, he created a moment in my life I will never forget. We built something awesome. He taught me the value of hard work. Building that ramp taught me that the more you invest in an experience the more opportunity you have to enjoy and appreciate it. I became proficient at cutting wood with a circular saw. I got efficient at drilling holes and screwing screws into the wood. I also learned through experience the wise adage, "Measure twice, cut once."

Later, when I was in high school, I gave a presentation on buoyancy. If you don't know what buoyancy is, I didn't either. In a nutshell, it means the ability of an object to float in water, air or some other medium.

The question framing this presentation was this: Could concrete float?

My initial thought when I first read the question was, "no," but that quickly changed as I understood the project more and saw the experiment in action. The funny thing is, I later discovered that when my father was in college studying to be an engineer, he'd made a concrete canoe to race against other engineering schools.

To teach me the principles surrounding buoyancy we set up a little lab in his workshop. We made specific molds, poured the concrete in and then watched specific shapes take form. We measured, cut, glued and screwed the different shapes. We mixed, poured and vibrated the concrete to better take on the properties of the shapes.

The different shapes illustrate Archimedes' principle of fluid mechanics that states, "A body while wholly or partially immersed in a fluid apparently loses weight by an amount equal to that of the fluid displaced." I'm a visual and kinesthetic learner and so I remember my dad explaining Archimedes' principle, but it was not until I'd built the different shapes and had seen the real-life results that I began to understand what it really meant.

As a kid, my father brought things to life and created unforgettable experiences. I want to do that for my kids, too. And I want to do that for other men to help them show up more powerfully and authentically.

My promise to you is that by the time you have read this book, you will have established an awareness of legacy, discovered your vision for your legacy, aligned with the purpose of your legacy, crafted a process to live your legacy, and understood how to best implement your process. This will allow you to create the impact you want for yourself, your family, your community and in the world.

The Legacy Code is a resource to discover your life's mission, its purpose, and to provide you with a catalyst for making it a reality. This won't happen by osmosis, you must be wiling to do the work. No one will do it for you. As a coach, I can help you speed up this process, but the work needs to be done by you.

This is a book that was specifically written to help you start living your legacy now, to enjoy your legacy, and to learn how to craft it purposefully so when you are gone, you will know deep down in your heart you have left a legacy that will make you proud. When your time comes, you'll not only know you will be leaving a legacy that inspires and impacts others but that you also lived it out daily.

Too often as men, we get sucked into chasing success in the, "I'm going to make a million dollars" or "I am going to achieve this goal," and we lose sight of the bigger vision of how it all will play out. We focus on instant gratification or what we think we should be doing to keep up with the Joneses. But legacy is so much bigger than success.

Here's a way to conceptualize the difference between the way most men think about success versus my invitation for you to rethink legacy. Success is loading a bag with other people's stuff, and the stuff you think you need. Eventually, that bag will weigh you down, slow you down and become exhausting.

Legacy however, is like a huge magnet pulling you toward it. The effort is minimal because a force greater than you drives you.

31

Your legacy can happen by accident, with no intent, no purpose, and not necessarily be positive or something you're proud of. My guess is if you're reading this you'd like to have a hand in creating your legacy. You'd like to be more purposeful. You'd like to use specific intent in crafting the legacy you want to live and the legacy you leave. If that is you, you are in the right place. The Legacy Code was designed with you in mind. It was designed to help you create your blueprint, to chart your roadmap, so you can take actions today to create your legacy of tomorrow.

Let's do this.

SECTION 1 – AWARENESS

CHAPTER 1: THE END

"Be ashamed to die until you've scored a victory for humanity."

- Horace Mann

You walk into the room, and people all around you are mourning and crying. You don't' know why. Then you see your kids, and they are crying. You see your wife, and she's crying, too. In the middle of the room is a casket. As you get closer, you see a man lying inside, it's you.

Picture this scenario now.

You are there, witnessing your wake, as people mourn over you. Your family is there. Ask yourself, if this were really you today, would you be happy with how you lived your life and with the impact your life had and will continue to have in the world? Would you feel fulfilled about the tools and experiences you left your kids? Would you be happy with the life you'd created for yourself and your wife?

When that time comes, it will be too late to ask these questions. Anything you could have done won't matter because you didn't do it. Today, as you read this, you have the luxury of stepping into that moment, going to the end and evaluating. You get to catch a glimpse of what your life could be like, what you would like to live out in your life.

Imagine your wife or future wife standing up in front of everyone to give your eulogy. She's sharing the impact you made in her life and is describing the man she knew you to be, what she saw day in and day out. She is describing how she will remember you and is reminiscing of the experiences you had together.

What would you want her to say?

What would you want her to feel?

These are simple, straightforward questions, but ensuring she will say those things and feel how you'd like her to will take some work. This is not the kind of thing that happens over night but the type of work that must be done daily.

If you haven't yet done so, take out some paper and answer these questions. The process may be a bit painful and yet I can guarantee it will impact your life positively. There are no "right" or "wrong" answers and what you write now does not have to be your final answers. This is just a starting place. By just writing down your genuine gut feeling, this exercise will help you establish a realistic starting point as you go through this journey. By the end of this book, you'll have an opportunity to go through this exercise again. There's a good chance you will want to revise your answers as you gain insight and that is part of this journey. Make sure you answer the questions now before you proceed.

Let's shift things a bit. Take a moment and think of one of your kids saying your eulogy. What would you hope him or her to say? What would you want him or her to feel? What life lessons would you want to have taught your kids? What experiences would you have had together, laughed about, and cried about together? What would you like that to look like?

Write down that experience. Again, go with your gut and move quickly through this.

Finally, imagine a close friend sharing your eulogy. What would you want your friend to say about you? What would you want your friend to say about your vision and the impact you made in his or her life and to the world?

Answer these questions now and then put your answers aside to save for later.

This may seem like a somber exercise to do, but when you complete it, you'll discover the clarity and transformation it can have on your life.

Hindsight is 20-20. Steve Jobs, Co-Founder of Apple Inc., said, "You can't connect the dots looking forward; you can only connect them looking backward. So, you need to trust that the dots will somehow connect in your future. You have to trust in something—your gut, destiny, life, karma, whatever. This approach has never let me down, and it has made all the difference in my life."

This exercise allows you to fast forward to the future you'd like to create; it gives you a way of looking back at the dots you need to connect to get there.

We are not immortal. We will all die. It doesn't matter how healthy we are, what supplements we take, the prayers we've said, or the people we've helped. The finality of life is what makes it so valuable and so amazing. Knowing how you want to live your life and connecting with the people that matter most in your life is imperative to living a purposeful and powerful legacy.

As you read this book, you will discover it is important to live a life that is truly rich and fulfilled, one that permits you to create an impact that matters.

In our society, there are too many men going through the motions. They've fallen into being comfortable and average. They've become like many other men around them: living without clarity, passion, or vision.

The great Renaissance painter Michelangelo of the Sistine Chapel in Italy said, "The greater danger for most of us lies not in setting our aim too high and falling short; but in setting our aim too low, and achieving our mark." Many men are afraid to reach for their potential because they are afraid to fail. Many men are afraid to reach for their visions because they don't feel worthy enough for that legacy. Perhaps this is you. As you go on this journey, permit yourself to walk in that fear, in that uncertainty, in that struggle. If you do that you will come out on the other side of being a R.I.C.H. Man. (I will explain what R.I.C.H. means in the upcoming chapters).

The Legacy Code is here to provide more clarity, guidance, and direction, surrounding the power of legacy. Legacy is greater than gold; it is not a thing but an impact on the people who experience it. Your legacy can serve others long after you are gone as a platform from which they can see, grow and further impact the world. Isaac Newton said, "If I have seen so far it is because I have stood on the shoulders of giants."

You can live your life and leave a legacy like a casino game where you simply roll the dice and leave it all up to chance or you can choose to live purposefully moving towards a vision of your choosing. Let's create that powerful and purposeful legacy that is yearning to come out. Let's create a legacy that will inspire you daily and serve as a shoulder for others to stand on long after you are gone.

CHAPTER 2: LEGACY REVEALED

"True leaders don't invest in buildings. Jesus never built a building. They invest in people. Why? Because success without a successor is failure. So, your legacy should not be in buildings, programs, or projects; your legacy must be in people."

- Myles Munroe

There he was competing in the Great Floridian Ironman Triathlon, both hips rubbing bone on bone. I remember seeing the pain and anguish on his face with each step. I had grown up running with him. I knew when he was in a good place and when he was in a bad place. I knew from the first step; this race would be a suffer-fest. I had never seen him run that slowly. It churned my stomach to watch him this way. How he shuffled down the road with a grimace transmitting the pain of each step to me. I had seen my father run many races, but I had never seen him not finish. I was scared he'd stop this time. Who would have blamed him? Not me.

It was late in the day. He had already swum 2.4 miles, biked 112 miles, and now he was in the process of running 26.2 miles to finish it off. Each mile, each minute, each step was a test of perseverance. My siblings and I cheered him on and ran next to him to keep him going. Exactly 12 hours and 21 minutes after he started, he crossed the finish line as an Ironman.

Photo Credit: Author

My father crossing the line of his Ironman in a time of 12:21:01. After this he'd go on to have bilateral hip resurfacing.

Business coach, artist, and urban monk Jamie Treadwell described legacy with this analogy. "Legacy is when you walk away. It's what is left for others to discover. Perhaps it's a memory, a lesson, an idea, or even an experience." That definition of legacy really resonates with me, especially when I remember my father on that day, stretching his physical limitations.

My father gave me a blueprint of perseverance and adventure even when the odds were stacked against him. He inspired a desire to push further than I ever thought possible no matter the circumstances. On that day, he reinforced it didn't matter what life threw my way if I was willing to put one step in front of the other I'd get to the end. I'd finish. I'd come out a stronger man, too. As you go through this process, focus on putting one step in front of the other even if and when it gets tough. One step at a time will get you there.

Legacy is like a rock dropped into the ocean. It creates ripples that travel beyond where you initially dropped the rock.

What is a Powerful, Purposeful Legacy?

One thing I noticed in all the interviews I conducted was that the men I talked to all had a different definition for legacy. Each had his own unique version that made sense to him. A big overarching theme especially among the fathers was that legacy was what they'd teach and leave their kids with once they were gone.

My personal definition for a powerful, purposeful legacy is:

The actions I take daily that align with my values and my vision that help me to grow and to positively impact the people around me and the generations to come when I'm gone.

Here's why I love this. It's something that's very purposeful. It's not a dream. It's not something I passively wish for. I am looking at my legacy as a proactive investment of time, energy, money, experiences and people. It allows me to create my legacy now with my daily actions.

Whenever I do or say anything, I strive to create a positive impact that will not only serve me now, and in the future, but that will also serve my family and my community.

Here's the quotable definition I created for my clients that means exactly what I described above, but is less cumbersome and easier to carry around with you when thinking about legacy: **"The life you live is the legacy you leave!"**

Write down how you are investing your time for the next week. Will these actions pave the way for you to leave the power of exponential growth in your future and beyond?

Your legacy is an ongoing journey that continues to evolve and grow and has the potential to live on long after you die. The deeper you impact someone or the number of people you touch both create the momentum for your legacy to continue long after you are gone.

Imagine a steep, tall mountain and a little hill. At the top of each one is a ball. You let the balls go. Which one is going to pick up more speed?

Which one will go further?

We know the right answer is the ball let go from the tall mountain. The more precise, more polarizing your vision, the taller your mountain and so the clearer it will be to define your legacy. The more momentum you create by rolling down the taller mountain, AKA - living out your vision, the longer that ball will keep rolling—the farther that ball will go.

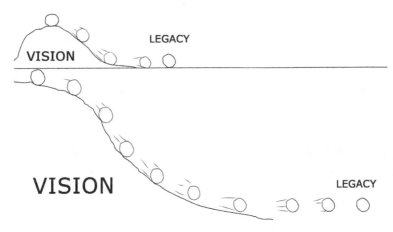

Photo Credit: Mhiz_wendy

Now it's your turn.

Let's dive in deep and define what a powerful and purposeful legacy means to you.

How do you define it?

What is it not?

How do you know if you are living out that legacy truthfully today?

49

Don't make it perfect but write something down. As you go through this book, you will continue to sculpt it. This will give you a starting point to work with.

Take out a piece of paper and write:

Legacy is...

Now finish that sentence. Another way of saying it is,

"I define legacy as..."

Perhaps you may have trouble defining what legacy is to you and so understanding what legacy *is not* will help you pinpoint a clearer, more vibrant picture of legacy.

For example, I know for a fact that legacy for me is not about achievement. Legacy is not about the accumulation of the most "things." Legacy is not about having the most expensive car or the biggest house. I am very clear about what it is not for me. That is what I want you to figure out as well for you.

Now finish this sentence:

"Legacy is not..."

The answers to these questions and statements give you a direction to start working towards. If you haven't done so, write down your answers now.

CHAPTER 3: A TALE OF TWO LEGACIES

"My own career reflects a strange dichotomy between the world we've long known and the world that will become."

– Jeffrey Toobin

There are two types of legacies that I want you to consider when you are thinking about legacy. One is your Personal Legacy and the other is your Impact Legacy. Through my conversations and interviews with men, I noticed that many men think they can only create either a Personal Legacy or Impact Legacy but not both. The good news is that this is a misconception and you can actually create both.

It is important to understand that you will always have the opportunity to make the most of both of these types of legacies. The extent of the ripples they make is determined by the conviction and consistency of your actions.

The two types of legacies are:

1) Personal Legacy

2) Impact Legacy.

Your Personal Legacy is determined by who you are as a person and the way you relate with and treat the people in your life: your inner circle of friends and family, the people who know you well, the people who you interact with most on a day-to-day basis, and even how you treat a stranger.

Sir Isaac Newton said, "If I've seen further it is because I've stood on the shoulders of giants." Your Impact Legacy is "the shoulders" you leave for others to stand on and build from. It may be the outcome of mastery in a specific area that allows the world to be better place.

Here's a great example of both. Steve Jobs left a powerful Impact Legacy. I would probably say most people have been influenced and affected by Steve Jobs in one way or another. Whether you have an Apple product or someone you know has one, his company created a ripple effect in our current society. He created something that became a lifestyle, and a movement, and all through a product that is essentially a commodity. He inspired people to associate and connect with his inventions on an emotional level. He took things like a music player, a computer, and a phone, objects that had no life, and he breathed life into them. He invited people to connect with these technologies and use them on an emotional level. This was his brilliance, his gift, his Impact Legacy.

Unfortunately, despite the magnitude of his Impact Legacy, Steve Jobs' Personal Legacy suffered. If you look at the many videos, books, and articles written and made about him, the people he worked with most and those closest to him felt he was a jerk. They didn't enjoy the way he treated them. I never knew him, but this alienation and uncaring became his Personal Legacy.

His vision of what he wanted to create was greater than anyone else. People became a means to an end. They believed in his vision because of his conviction, leadership, ruthlessness, and clarity but his interactions left much to be desired.

It doesn't have to be an either/or decision. You have the possibility and capability to purposefully create both legacies. My personal belief and one shared by many of the men I've interviewed takes the form of a question: what good is the great business or foundation you started, a book or piece of music you've written if you've failed your family—the people who matter most in your life?

Start with gaining clarity around your personal legacy and staying congruent with it in all you say and do. This will lay a strong and stable foundation for an Impact Legacy that is fulfilling.

Impact Legacies that have longevity are distinct and definitive. They tend to be polarizing. Black and white leads to more clarity. The gray zone is forgettable.

We are aware of good and bad extremes. On one end, is Mother Teresa who made a stand and served the poorest of the poor with love, empathy, and compassion. In the beginning, she had very little support from the church and others. But as people saw the work and transformation happening in Calcutta, India they were drawn to it. She was doing the work not to reach fame or fortune but out of love and conviction. Her intention allowed her to continue serving during the darkest of times.

She started as a rebel because originally, the church didn't want her there. But that is where she felt called to serve, and that is part of creating a powerful and purposeful legacy. Follow your faith, your values, and your beliefs with such certainty you can't be ignored.

Be clear and committed to your beliefs. Let your "yes" mean "yes," and your "no" mean "no."

Have conviction in what you believe and what you don't believe. Stay true to that belief and act on it daily.

Mother Teresa didn't serve the poor for a week. She dedicated her whole life to serving because she believed and wanted to care for people to the greatest extent she could. She didn't do it for accolades or a pat on the back.

At the other end of the spectrum, there was Hitler. The world will never forget his demented view of humanity and his atrocious acts of violence. Why? Because he had an extremely demented but precise vision of his truth and he executed it. You see, the more committed in your beliefs and action you are, the greater the impact you'll leave, regardless of how good or bad, moral or immoral you are.

Imagine a sculptor working on a marble slab. When he selects his tools, first he uses a chisel to remove chunks of marble and cut deep crisp, defined lines on the marble. Once he is done chipping and removing the marble to reveal the masterpiece he uses sandpaper to smooth out and finish the surface. Most men live their lives using sandpaper on the surface when they haven't chiseled away all the marble covering the masterpiece. They live in the grey zone, that middle zone, between living a life unleashed and a life of obscurity. Use your chisel, make your sharp clear lines that are easy-to-follow to define your legacy.

Comedian, actor, musician, and author Steve Martin said, "Be so good they can't ignore you." The grey zone becomes forgettable, a commodity that is "here today and gone tomorrow."

Since you are reading these words, I can infer it's because you want more. Perhaps you want more certainty, more clarity, more direction, and more support in creating and living your legacy. Whatever it is, you have likely acknowledged there is a potential for your life that you have not fulfilled. Be courageous and begin living that potential. Potential that is not executed dies with you when you die but potential that is lived out, lives on long after you die.

Consider that you impact the world and yet the people that you love most never get the benefit of you in their lives. In other words, you can create a cure for cancer but never speak to your children, never speak to your wife, and never totally invest in yourself. While yes, you may go on to save millions of lives, which is commendable, my belief is that the people around you who matter the most in your life require that same kind of importance.

As men, our egos usually guide us to focus first on creating our Impact Legacy. Our ego wants everyone out there to know our greatness long after we are gone. Society re-enforces this belief with the glorification of men of power and achievement. French Revolution military leader

Napoleon Bonaparte said, "Power is my mistress. I have worked too hard at her conquest to allow anyone to take her away from me." That statement sums up the way many men approach life and their Impact Legacy. They focus on achieving no matter what it costs them or whom they hurt. In the end, they end up with the same question, "Is that all there is?"

What good is it to save the world but lose those who matter most to you? What I am saying is go ahead, find the cure to cancer and be present; be a part of the lives of the people who matter most in your life. If you focus on creating a solid Personal Legacy, one in which you experience both personal and family growth, it can serve as the seed from which your Impact Legacy can flourish from.

CHAPTER 4: TYRANNOSAURUS R.I.C.H.

"It takes a different values system if you wish to change the world."

– Jacque Fresco

I believe this could be one of the most important things you get clear on. I want to share the value system that has helped me significantly. It's called the R.I.C.H. Man Value System or the R.I.C.H. Man Experience. R.I.C.H. is an acronym for Respected, Inspired, Connected and Happy. Before I explain further, allow me to share how the R.I.C.H. Man Value System came to be.

In February of 2013, I had a deep uneasiness come upon me, my business, and my life. My fitness and physical therapy practice that I'd grown with love, passion, and purpose felt like an anchor pulling me down to the bottom of the ocean. I fell out of love with it. I knew I wanted to help others on a deeper more meaningful level, but I didn't know how to do it or what that possibility would even look like. Up to that point, I had been crystal clear on my path in life. In high school, I knew what I wanted to be, and I went after my dream in college. Then I graduated with my undergraduate degree in three years and went on to open my business, a sports performance and fitness training facility. All along my journey, I'd known exactly what each next step had to be.

Initially, I trained athletes to perform at their peak performance. Then I expanded my practice to training and helping working men and women. I found something amazing in each person I worked with, and I wanted to help each person reach his or her full potential. The idea of helping them reach their potential lit me up with excitement and purpose.

I opened my business in 2005. I was helping people improve their health, their performance, and their life and it was very fulfilling. Soon, I realized that I wanted to have a more lasting impact by helping my clients transform their lives on another level. I wanted to continue transforming their health, fitness, and bodies and now also their mindset. I wanted to dive deeper into understanding how I could affect people longer-term. But I felt trapped because I didn't know how to transition from the way I helped my clients. Not knowing left me feeling frustrated and like I was drowning.

Logically it did not make sense that I felt this way. I had a wonderful wife. We had 2 amazing children. We had a nice house. We had 2 cars. We had nothing to complain about. I was living the American dream. Still, I found myself asking, "Is that all there is?" Even though I had a successful business that helped people, I still felt empty, and it was sad to me. Something was missing. This feeling of uncertainty, frustration, and loss of hope took me to a dark place. I felt caged inside. I felt as if I was in a prison I'd created for myself. I am not sure if you've ever felt that way, but I can tell you it is not comforting nor empowering to believe you have created your own prison, your own struggles, and yet not know what to do about it. It was not just frustrating—it was demoralizing.

I was accustomed to knowing what I wanted

and how to get it. This was a new experience for me. It was shaking me to the core. My identity had been taken away.

Have you ever felt like your identity was stripped away from you?

I asked myself, *who am I now? What am I going to do?* Those were the thoughts going through my head that led me into a dark place. I fell into a deep depression. In fact, I would see clients in the morning and then go home and sleep for 4-6 hours. I didn't want to do anything. I stopped marketing the business. I just wanted it all to be gone.

At the time, my wife, Christian, was pregnant with our third child. Our business was quickly declining. We were having problems paying bills. Every day I'd wake up and feel lost and frustrated. Then one day, my friend, coach, and mentor, Dax reached out to me and invited me to go to an amazing retreat he was hosting in Thailand. At the time, we couldn't afford it because of where I had sunk our business. The other issue was Christian would be just a week shy of her due date during the retreat. That meant there was a good chance I would miss the birth of my son. I felt hopeless. I remember telling Christian about the retreat. I stared into her deep emerald eyes, embarrassed. She looked back at me with a confidence that rocked me to my core.

Every time I tell the story, I still get emotional and feel that pit in my stomach. Christian asked, "Do you feel this will help you get out of this funk?" I said "Yes!" What she said next is the greatest proclamation of love I've ever witnessed. I say this because of the situation and the certainty to which she responded. Imagine your 7-month-pregnant wife staring at you with her emerald green eyes saying, "I don't know how else to help you anymore. You need to do this. This baby is coming, and when that happens, I need you to be the man I know you to be. I need you to be the husband I know you to be. I want you to be the father I've seen you be. Don't do this for you but for us, for our family. We need you back."

I was completely shocked that she was courageous enough, even while seven months pregnant, to say those words to me. That moment was the catalyst that moved me toward to that retreat. To know that my wife had that much love and confidence in me was inspiring. That moment became the key to unlocking the shackles that held me prisoner.

I had not been showing up as the leader of my house, and I am grateful she led our family in that decision. If she had said, "No," I don't know what would have happened. I believe we would have figured it out but receiving her confidence, trust, and commitment allowed me the opportunity to show her I could be the leader of the family.

The day of the retreat finally arrived, April 16, 2014. I was flying across the world for the first time. The flight went from Miami to New York, then from New York to Shanghai. It was the longest flight I've ever taken. I went crazy in that plane and would pace up and down the aisles. I even jogged a bit and did stretches to keep me sane. When I finally arrived at Shanghai, there was a problem. Apparently, I had never gotten the information for the connecting flight to Phuket, Thailand. I explained my situation to the travel desk attendant, and she figured out a way to get me to Phuket on time. She told me there was only one flight left that day that was going to Phuket. It was across the airport and leaving in 15 minutes.

"I don't think you'll make it in time," the ticket agent said. I thanked her and told her I would. Then I got my ticket and started to run, my backpack bouncing up and down, as I dragged my carry-on luggage. I raced across the tarmac, through the gates, and up the escalators. My legs burned and all I could think about was, "I can't let my family down." I was thinking, "*I had flown this far, and now I was going to miss the first* day of the retreat if I didn't catch this flight." It was unacceptable. I kept reminding myself as I pushed my legs, "I have to make it." "I have to make it." "I have to make it." Then I heard, "Final call to Phuket." My ears perked up, and I dug in deep to race to the gate right before they closed the doors. I had done it. My legs were Jell-O, but I'd made it. Emotion flooded through me, and I felt as though life were asking, *do you want it badly enough?* I did!

I arrived at Phuket at 2 a.m. and luckily was able to crash with friends. At 6 a.m., I popped out of bed with a deep sense of gratitude. I put on my running shoes and went for an exploratory run. Every step I took was a reminder that I had made it. Now, it was time to do the work to ensure I showed up as the man, husband, father and leader to my family.

In Thailand, I gained massive clarity and perspective on my life. Part of it was the fact I was starting to live the life I wanted. I began by creating a morning routine that helps me start off my day inspired.

Have you ever been so brutally honest with yourself that it physically hurt?

In Thailand, during my coaching sessions and journaling work I realized how much I had let down my family, the most important people in the world to me. I realized that my not being the best version of myself was negatively impacting them. My wife had a watered-down version of her husband. She deserved so much more than that. My kids, whom I love to death, had a stranger for a father. It's not because I wasn't there physically but because I had checked out mentally. I was always thinking about work or finances. This was not the type of husband or father I wanted to be. I remember breaking down and crying in the living room of our villa and feeling a deep sense of remorse and sadness so heavy that it felt like I had a car on my chest. It was crushing.

On the flip side, have you ever dreamt so big you were overcome with joy? A dream so joyful it made you smile from ear to ear?

Two days after that breakdown in the villa during my coaching session, I accepted full responsibility for my actions. That ownership brought about the freedom needed to help me dream and create my greatest and grandest vision for the type of husband and father I wanted to become. It gave me the clarity around the personal and impact legacy I wanted to create and live out daily. I couldn't stop smiling. It was such an empowering feeling.

During the 10 days I was in Thailand, I experienced confusion, frustration, sadness, clarity, joy, excitement, inspiration and freedom all multiple times a day. I realized there was nothing wrong with my fitness and physical therapy practice. In fact, it was unique, the only business of its kind. My wife and I had created an environment, for our clients, that was truly special. Once I recognized this, it gave me a renewed sense of pride and purpose.

Remember when I asked if you've ever dreamt so big you couldn't help but smile? That is what happened next. During the retreat, I had the space and guidance to explore and create a program that I found deep purpose and mission in. I recognized there were other men just like me: family-centered entrepreneurial men who were going through similar feelings and experiences like the ones I had gone through. As a result, I created the program I wished I'd had access to that addressed the different areas of my life that I had been struggling with. Once I designed this program, I named it the R.I.C.H. Man Experience. The mission of the R.I.C.H. Man Experience is to help married men show up powerfully in their marriage, health, and business, and to create a clear vision and inspiring legacy. It's a program based off rock solid values to ensure you can show up as the best version of yourself daily.

That retreat in Thailand forever changed the trajectory of my life.

I designed and created the R.I.C.H. Man Experience. The retreat ended. I flew back home and three days later I was with my wife as she gave birth to our third child. Since then, I've been showing up more powerfully as a husband, father, and man. I've been coaching married men to do the same and helping them create their own inspiring legacy.

Becoming a rich man took on a new definition for me. Most people think of rich in the context of someone who has lots of money. I have redefined it as a value system that has since become a compass to guide men everywhere how to show up more powerfully in their lives.

Let me remind you what R.I.C.H. stands for: Respected, Inspired, Connected, and Happy.

The R.I.C.H. Man value system allowed me to

confidently know the direction and actions I wanted to take. With the discovery and implementation of this value system, I now have the conviction to decide what I say yes to and no to confidently.

Let's explore the R.I.C.H. Man value system for a moment so you can get an idea of the clarity it can bring in your life: to become a man operating under the values of being R.I.C.H. - Respected, Inspired, Connected, and Happy.

I define respected as a man with compassion who keeps his composure and controls his emotions. He is effective and efficient. He is truthful and honest.

Let's get clear, ask yourself the following questions:

- What does it mean for you to show up as a man who is respected?
- What daily practices would need to be true

for you to show up as a respected man?

- How do you need to show up so that you are someone that is respected by others?

The second component of the R.I.C.H. value system is Inspired. Most people talk about motivation, but motivation is short-lived. Motivation is an external stimulus to help push you forward. Inspiration is an internal energy that brings out your light. It means quite literally to be filled with the spirit. Imagine becoming a beacon of light. When you come from a place of inspiration, you become a lighthouse. You shine a light on everything else to illuminate the way. You are bursting from the inside out.

Motivation is looking for the light source, while inspiration is becoming the light source to confidently guide you and others in any circumstance or struggle. In order to become that light source you must be congruent with your values and beliefs.

Ask yourself, *how can I come from a place of inspiration to serve others?*

The next value is Connected.

Being connected to yourself, your family, your business, your purpose, and your contribution allows you to show up more powerfully.

So, how can you be more connected in each and every situation? Ask yourself, *am I showing up as someone who is connected right now in this situation?* If the answer is no, then ask yourself, *"How can I connect in this moment?*

Let me share an example. I had a long day at work, plus I trained really early so I was tired and needed time for me. The kids hadn't seen me all day. Normally I would have just been either in a bad mood or would have locked myself in my room. Before I went inside the house I asked, "How can I connect with the best version of myself and spend time with the kids?" When I came in I hugged and kissed my wife and kids. I let them know I needed to be in nature to recharge. I invited them to go on an adventure with me. They loved it because we went on an adventure in the park next to our house and I got to recharge in nature as well as spend time with them.

- How can you connect with the best part of you?
- How can you better connect with those around you?

The final value is Happy. Happiness is not something we achieve but something we reveal. It is something we go inward for, not outward.

I remember in college I obsessed about every little thing regarding my training. Whether I'd have a good or bad race I'd find something to be upset about. I remember my father telling me, "You are so lucky to be doing this [running in college] and you are wasting so much time and energy being upset."

Talk about a wake-up call.

I had the privilege to be a collegiate athlete and I was missing it all because I chose to focus on the mistakes and never celebrate the victories. That changed when I decided to embrace gratitude. Now every opportunity I got to run was a celebration of the process. I was happier, my training got better and so did my results. When I embraced the present and the process with gratitude the rest took care of itself.

Who do I need to become to be happy?

Remember the R.I.C.H. Man value system acronym stands for RESPECTED, INSPIRED, CONNECTED, HAPPY. Use this or your clearly defined value system as a compass. Have it direct your actions so that they align with your vision, purpose, and process to create your purposeful and powerful legacy.

When times get rough, you will have an asset in your value system to provide a way to overcome it. Times will get tough when you are pushing the boundaries and growing daily. Using R.I.C.H. as a compass will guide you out of those choppy waters with more certainty. You will have more strength, more endurance, and more resolve to navigate through because you will be clearer on who you are and who you need to be to create a legacy that inspires and ignites you.

In the past, I'd get distracted by the latest new strategy or tool I was supposed to be using in my business instead of what most aligned with my values. Now using the R.I.C.H. Man Value System I have a compass to ensure my actions, tools, and strategies stay aligned with what I believe to best serve my clients, my family, and myself.

CHAPTER 5: DARKSIDE OF LEGACY

"People are chasing cash, not happiness. When you chase money, you're going to lose. You're just going to. Even if you get the money, you're not going to be happy."

– Gary Vaynerchuk

It was February 6, 2001, my junior year in college. I had been training all winter break running twice a day Monday through Saturday, including a 2-hour run on Sunday. I was eating every 2-3 hours because my metabolism was a furnace instantly burning anything that came its way. I was in the best running shape of my life. I had dropped down to 135 pounds from my normal 148 pounds, and my body fat percentage teetered between 3-4 percent. I felt lean and fast.

Photo Credit: Author
Armando, sprinting to the finish line at a University of Miami track meet.

It was our third track practice as a team. The workout was 4x 1mile with a 2-minute rest in between. Right from the start, I took my place at the front of the pack. I led them through all four laps and crossed the first mile in 4 minutes 48 seconds. After two-minutes of rest, we were off. Again, I took the lead and towed the group to a 4:49. My legs felt good. My ego felt great. Up until that day I'd always found myself in the middle or back of the pack. This was my first time leading the workouts.

On my third set, I felt something weird on my right foot, but I pushed ahead and finished in 4:48. As I was waiting to begin our final interval, I limped on that foot. I remember having this conversation in my head: *you should stop, something is not right.* I shook off that idea and responded to myself; this is the best workout you've ever done. In a race, if you have pain or feel discomfort, are you going to stop? Hell no! This is training for those *exact moments. Suck it up and finish this workout.*

That is exactly what I did. After the first few bothersome steps, I found my groove. My endorphins buzzed and my legs moved along. I led the pack for the final time of 4:49, feeling on top of the world. I had never run so nimbly. The many hours I had put in practicing had finally paid off.

I went to do a cool down run, but as soon as I took the first step, sharp debilitating pain shot through my foot. I fell to the floor. The athletic trainer came to inspect what had happened. I was instructed to ice and rest my foot for three days.

After a few days of rest and hobbling through school, I tried to run again. The sharp pain persisted. I had to go to the doctor and see what was going on. It was bad news. The x-ray showed a stress fracture in my right foot. All that I had worked for, all my hopes for the season were crushed.

Understanding your body's thresholds and the consequences of crossing them is a valuable lesson I learned. One of the consequences of dropping below 4 percent body fat is that it starts affecting your hormones. At 3-4 percent, it affected my bone density, and you know how that turned out.

We've talked a lot about the power and benefits of legacy but are there any pitfalls or consequences of chasing legacy?

Yes.

The pitfall of chasing a legacy is the same pitfall of chasing success or achievement. You are always chasing, meaning you are *always behind*. That is why I make the distinction to create your legacy, not chase it. Creating puts you in the driver's seat to plan, respond, and live.

Legacy often gets mistaken for achievement. Your achievements will be part of your legacy, but when you use achievement as evidence of your worthiness, happiness, or fulfillment, you will come up short every time. Similar to my running, I was chasing faster times instead of celebrating each step and being aware of the man I had become.

The long-term problem with achievement when it is tied to your worth is that once you get there, you realize there is another achievement or another finish line you feel compelled to reach. Just so I am clear achieving goals is important. Achieving goals helps you grow but it does not define you nor give you your worth. You will never feel long-term happiness and fulfillment chasing achievement.

If you are looking for happiness or fulfillment, you will not find it outside of yourself, but rather, to find it you need to go inward. If you can't be happy and fulfilled right now, then no matter how many achievements or successes you obtain, you will never be happy or satisfied.

Happiness and fulfillment are two very different things than achievement. Happiness and fulfillment is what is revealed when you align your values and beliefs to your Legacy Code. Achievements help to amplify your legacy only when they align with your values and beliefs.

If you have no idea how to be happy or how to come from a place of happiness, start with gratitude.

Think of three things you are grateful for and write down why they are important to you.

If you are still unclear, ask, *how can I serve others right now and bring them joy?*

You'll start seeing things differently. The truth will be revealed to you, and it will provide you with more direction.

I suggest that if you want to leave a powerful and purposeful Personal Legacy, you must first become clear with your values. Your values become your compass to allow you to always find your way.

If you are unsure of your values use the R.I.C.H. Man Value system (Respected, Inspired, Connected, Happy) in chapter 4. Review their definitions. Practice using them in any situation to help guide and direct you in your decisions.

The R.I.C.H. Man Values System is the system I created for my clients and myself. It has proved to be a great starting point.

If you wish to go deeper and create your own customized value system I walk you through that process at www.LegacyCodeBook.com/yourlegacy

If you are not operating in alignment with your values, then you won't be operating as the greatest and grandest version you are capable of.

Imagine that you and I are going to race cars. We have the same exact car, and the same amount of gas, the same amount of roadway, but I have eight cylinders, and you only have two cylinders firing, instead of the eight. Who is going to perform better, and go faster? I will win because I have six extra cylinders working for me. Your capacity is there; your potential is there, but you can't access it. This is just an analogy, but the reality is you are not racing anyone. It is just you. If you have an 8-cylinder capacity, ask yourself if you are okay just living out a 2-cylinder life and leaving a 2-cylinder legacy?

Since you are reading this book, I want to assume that your answer is no. In order to live your 8-cylinder life and leave your 8-cylinder legacy, create and implement Your Legacy Code.

SECTION 2 – YOUR VISION

CHAPTER 6: MY EYES DO NOT SEE

"Just because a man lacks the use of his eyes doesn't mean he lacks vision."

– Stevie Wonder

It was my sophomore year at FIU. I was in one of my athletic training classes. We were on a 10-minute break, and it was 10 in the morning. I was hungry, so I took out my lunch: leftover rice, spinach, and steak. After eating, I remember walking into class feeling a little bit off. I asked the teacher if there was something wrong with my eyes or my face. She said, "No."

When class finished, I had to walk across campus to get to my car. By that time, I was seeing double. When you simultaneously see two images, you don't know where to look. It was hard to balance. I couldn't walk straight. I staggered across the university parking lot. I kept running into the parked cars. It was scary. I remember thinking, *what is going on?* I felt out of control.

As an athlete, I had complete dominance of how I moved my body. Now all the rules for movement were different, and it was surreal. Everything that I had known visually was completely unreliable. When I got to my car, I called my mom and told her I was seeing double. I asked if she thought it would be a good idea if I drove home. Like a smart mom, she said, "No, I'm going to pick you up and take you to the hospital to get you checked out." I didn't want her to miss work and I didn't want to go to the hospital. I have always been in phenomenal health, so I thought whatever it was would pass, and that it was probably nothing. She said, "You know, I'd rather be wrong, take time off, and find out we have nothing to worry about."

The doctors informed my mom and I that my brainstem was swollen but they didn't know why. They were concerned and thought I had multiple sclerosis (MS). Test after test came up inconclusive. At this point in my life, I was a collegiate runner, studying to be an athletic trainer and an exercise physiologist. Everything I did involved being physical.

The doctors wanted to address my swollen

brainstem, so they started pumping me with corticosteroids to decrease the inflammation. They still weren't sure if I had MS.

Imagine being told you have a destructive autoimmune disease that renders you so weak you can't even breathe. I was scared. All my dreams, everything I'd envisioned for my life involved my being physical. I had never envisioned being trapped in my own body.

The uncertainty was draining. I lived in fear that everything I had worked for, everything I thought my life was going to be changed in the blink of an eye. I remember for multiple months, taking those steroids and being unable to focus on anything. I couldn't use my eyes properly, and I realized how many ways I depended on them. I needed my eyes. Everything I was good at, everything that I appreciated, it all depended on my eyesight. Not having vision will completely change your life. That is what I experienced for a few months of my life.

After a few months of testing, the doctors concluded I didn't have MS. It wasn't anything that they had ever seen. They couldn't explain why my brainstem swelled up or even if it would happen again. They said it was idiopathic. If you have no idea what that means, neither did I. I asked one of the nice doctors what it meant. He looked over his shoulder to make sure no one was around. He came in closer and with a mischievous smile he whispered, "Idiopathic is the medical term we use when we have no idea why something happened." His honesty brought a smile on my face and taught me two things: 1) don't take life so seriously and 2) enjoy the moments you have now, because you have no idea what the future brings.

I find that too many men go through life blind to what they want their legacy to be. As a result, they stumble through life like I had stumbled into the parked cars that day. They walk around not seeming to get anywhere because they lack vision. Most days feel like Groundhog Day. They lack drive and intention because they don't have clarity of vision. They just clock in and clock out sedated by the distractions of this world.

They gamble with their legacy.

I found out twice, first, when my vision was messed up and second, when I went to Thailand, that a life without vision is difficult and not the way I want to live. I feel that too many men haven't even had the opportunity or the guidance to help show them what their life could be like with a clear vision.

CHAPTER 7: FIND LIGHT IN THE DARK

"A great man is a torch in the darkness, a beacon in superstition's night, an inspiration, and a prophecy."

– Robert Green Ingersoll

Have you ever been taught something, but you couldn't quite grasp it until it was presented to you in a completely different way, and then it made total sense?

When I was in Thailand on the retreat trying to get my life back together, part of my process involved taking morning runs. I'd pray and meditate. I'd journal in different environments. My coach would guide us through strategic questions designed to peel back the layers of how we really felt and who we really were. He encouraged us to use the beauty of the beach, the pools, the landscape and the villas to tap into our most authentic self. He shared that our environment is the biggest predictor of our actions and thoughts. My tendency when I try to work is to lock myself in a room and go to work. I decided to embrace what my coach had suggested about leveraging the environment. I worked through my thoughts in the villas, by the pools, on the beach, and in the grass. I was blown away by the access to creativity and clarity of thought. It was as if I had tapped into a river of thoughts, feelings and visions that made my life better.

The reason I was in Thailand on this retreat was because my wife was pregnant with our third child; we were struggling financially, I had fallen out of love with my business, and I felt like an imposter to my wife, my kids and my clients. I wanted something else, something more but I had no clue what that something else was.

My coach asked me to write, "What is the life and legacy that you'd like to leave?" I wrote down the question but had no clue how to answer it. Trying to resolve that question was exactly why I'd flown across the world. I was so overwhelmed in that moment that I suspected anything I said or wrote would probably be wrong.

Have you ever felt overwhelmed, frustrated, and even scared that anything you did would probably be wrong?

My coach saw I was stuck and wasn't progressing, so he did what is called a pattern interrupt. He said, "You are dead. Your wife is giving your eulogy. What would you want her to say about you? What would you want her to know beyond a shadow of a doubt? What would you want her to experience while you were alive? What would you need to have done to feel that your time here on earth was important?" He helped me step into my future using a visceral situation.

Wow!

It was like being kicked right in the gut with his big combat boot. He had just unlocked what I needed. I was overcome with emotion as I wrote it out. I was becoming clearer on exactly what I wanted and why it was important to me.

As with all master coaches, they know when to

hold off and let you be with your struggle and when it's time to peel back another layer. As I finished writing, he said, "Now go deeper and think about your son or daughter sharing your eulogy. What kind of father, what kind of man, would you want them to say you were? What would you want them to say about the impact you had on this world?"

Again, he sent me down an amazing vortex of emotions ranging from happy to excited to inspired to proud. It was such an empowering experience to step into that moment at the end and look back at the life I'd created. Different types of relationships in our lives are privy to different facets of who we are. The experience of the legacy you leave your children will be a little different than the one your wife experiences and different than the ones your friends experience.

I wrote three eulogies from three different vantage points.

First, I wrote as if my wife were eulogizing me. Then, I wrote a eulogy as if my oldest son were going to give it. Finally, I wrote one that would sound like a friend giving my eulogy.

I mentioned before that I think your Personal Legacy takes precedence and is the foundation above anything else. Your Personal Legacy deals with those people, things, and experiences that matter most to you. It deals with those closest to you, those who love you. When you start there, it creates stable ground to move forward powerfully in your Impact Legacy.

Now it is your turn.

In this section of the book, let's create your vision and gain absolute clarity on what you want your legacy to be.

Later we will use this vision to help you create a process to help you live it out.

Answer these questions:

- What is the kind of life and impact I want to create for my family?
- What is the type of person I want to be and how do I want to influence people?
- What kind of work do I want to be doing and how do I want it to bring value to other people's life?
- What kind of impact or gift do I want to leave in this world?

Now answer these questions using your wife and kids for context:

- What is important that they know today?
- What does that say about me?

If you are finding it difficult to visualize what you want, consider:

- What and who brings joy to your life?
- What or who would break your heart if they

weren't in your life?

After you think about that, I want you to think about *what it is costing you not to fulfill that legacy.*

- *Who loses out?*
- *What are the effects of that legacy not being realized, to yourself, to those closest to you?*

As with most things in life, you will get what you put into it. If all you are doing is reading and nodding your head "yes," but you are not doing the work, then these exercises and your lack of action will not help you. Invest this time in you. I know it is difficult to go through this process by yourself. There is nothing like the power of having a coach right next to you. I see it daily with my clients and have personally experienced the power of leveraging a coach in this process. Allow me to be that coach for you and guide you.

Get FREE access to a special course that will walk you through the legacy creation process. I created this course just for you since you are reading this book. Visit www.LegacyCodeBook.com/yourlegacy

Let me share something intimate. What follows is the example of my son eulogizing me that I wrote when I was in Thailand. Even now as I step into that moment, my heart is filled with emotions. Enjoy:

> "Thank you all for coming to pay your respects to Armando Cruz, a man who changed the lives of so many people he came into contact with. This man was an inspiration, a leader, my best friend, and most of all, an amazing father. I grew up very fortunate to have such a great example of what it means to be a real man. My brothers and sisters and I learned the fundamentals of how to treat others

and serve them; we learned how to have a loving and fruitful marriage. We learned what being R.I.C.H. really is. He taught us that to be truly R.I.C.H., you must have connection. Man, could he connect with us. He always found ways to make us feel special and really pay attention to us as kids. He would attend our events, yes. But daily, he found a way to connect with us in the way we wanted. Sometimes we'd go on crazy adventures. He loved surprises but struggled to keep them for too long because he would get so excited. That is the loving energy he brought into every situation. He taught us to live our lives to the fullest, in order to serve the most people. He taught us to love each other and ourselves. He taught us to love the little things. He taught us to play and keep that joy, curiosity, and wonder of a child. He taught us always to have a sense of adventure, and that with every adventure there lies a treasure inside. Sometimes, you learn things about each other, other times about yourself in these adventures. Still, other times, you'd learn a new skill or data that nature taught. He taught us to be producers, not consumers; he taught us to respect others and ourselves. He taught us to have faith in people. He felt people were inherently good and one of his favorite quotes was by Goethe. He said, "See a man for the way he is, and he stays as he is. See a man for what he ought to be and can be and he becomes what he ought to be and can be."

This really sums up the way my father saw others. He had the ability to see greatness inside each person. I feel fortunate to witness that every day. People often come up to me and thank me for how my dad helped them to transform their marriage, their life, their health, and their business.

He taught people how to love themselves

and how to use that love to serve others and produce value in this world. Today, I am sad because we lost such a great man. I am sad because I lost my best friend. I am sad because I lost the best dad a son could ask for.

Here is the thing that brings me joy. I get to see the bits and pieces of my father in each and every person he came into contact with. The spark inside them is his signature trademark. Never forget your sparkle and share it with others every single day. Thank you for being part of his life. Thank you for sharing your deep and touching stories of how he changed your life with me. He received so much from each person here. Whether you know it or not, you had an impact on his life. He had the ability to appreciate the little things that may seem insignificant but made the difference to him. Thank you for coming and celebrating his life with us. My only request is that you live honestly and authentically and don't lose that sparkle inside that lets the world know they are meeting the real you."

That's what I wrote when I was in Thailand in 2014. I would love for my son to say it on the day I die. The reason it is important to me is because if he said that I'd know, I would have left a legacy of which I could be proud. Each one of the words I wrote contains different components of how I try to live my life. I let my kids know. I let my wife know. I let the people who I connect with know they matter, that they are worth it. That's my mission. It is the reason I was put on this earth. I believe that with all my heart.

When you show up as the most honest and truest version of yourself in this world, the more you will produce and give to this world. So, as a man, I believe that being the best man, the best father, the best person, and the best leader you can be, will greatly impact this world. Because the people you come into contact with will never be the same after meeting the truest and best version of you.

In the first chapter I invited you to write your eulogy and asked you to set it aside. Since then we've gone over the different types of legacies, the power of purposefully creating your legacy, understanding and applying the R.I.C.H. Man values system, and the positive impact being clear on your vision can have in your life. Now write your eulogy through at least one of the following: the eyes of your kids, the eyes of your wife, the eyes of a friend, the eyes of an acquaintance and/or someone who only met you once.

If someone met you once, what kind of impact would you like to leave in his or her life?

- What would you want them to take away from any experience with you?
- Write down why it's important to you.

- What is your belief? Who is missing out if you don't show up as the greatest and grandest version of yourself?

After you are done writing you can compare the original to this one to see the growth that has happened in such a short time.

If you'd like my help walking through these steps, I've created a FREE course that walks you through that process. Simply go to www.LegacyCodeBook.com/yourlegacy

SECTION 3 – YOUR PURPOSE

CHAPTER 8: FINDING PURPOSE – THE UNICORN

"I feel like a lot of people have a hard time finding what they want to do, or they have a job or career and not a passion. That's miserable for me. Just find your purpose; understand that you have one life to live."

– Trevor Jackson

Purpose: the unicorn of the personal development space. Everyone talks about the importance of finding your purpose, but few actually show you how. Part of the reason finding your purpose isn't taught is because there is not a clear-cut path. The other issue is that most men aren't willing to put in the work and be truthful with themselves.

I've talked to so many frustrated men who have this idea of how they should find their purpose. They say, "I get that it's important. I get that I need it, but I don't know how to find it." I empathize with you if you are in that position because I was there. I was frustrated trying to find my purpose. But that all changed when I realized I had been looking at it all wrong. The way we talk about purpose is as if we've lost a pair of shoes in the woods. Thinking of purpose in this way is a surefire route to frustration and to feeling as though you are a failure. Purpose is not something we lost "out there." It is something we have to reveal or discover inside ourselves. In other words, you must go inward to find purpose.

Purpose is the driving force or the why behind your vision. It is often interchanged with your reason for why you do something. You can find purpose in the passion that drives you, in the people who matter most, and in the impact, you want to leave.

Begin your discovery process with the following questions:

1.) What are three things, people, and experiences that matter most to me?

2.) Why are each of these important to me?

3.) Is there a way to combine any of these things, people, and experiences to make them stronger?

4.) As I read over these, which one am I naturally drawn to? Which one moves me most?

5.) Think of this like trying on a pair of sneakers. You try on multiple pairs to see which fits best. Then you walk, run, and jump around to see if they still feel good under more extreme conditions. Experiment using one of the experiences you selected above as your purpose for two weeks.

Here's an example on how to use this when you don't feel like doing something. When I don't feel like getting up at 3 a.m. to do my run I go back and remember how much I love the stillness, peace and tranquility of the morning. I remember how much I love the morning dew that sits on the trail as a blanket of fog rolls in. I remind myself how much better I feel once I've done something for me when most people are fast asleep. These reminders help shift my state and give me the strength to break free from the evil clutches of the warm cozy blanket monster trying to keep me in bed. If you've ever tried to get up early to train you understand what I mean.

I want you to experiment with different purposes. What you'll find is you'll have your big "P" Purpose and your little "p" purpose. Both are valuable tools. You may find a certain purpose may drive you more in some circumstances than it will in others. Take away judgment from this. Focus on embracing the process. Try on these purposes like you would a coat. If it fits, great, keep it. If it doesn't, find another one to try on.

It was a warm, humid evening. The sky was dark, and I was getting home from my collegiate track practice. My mother met me at the front porch of the house. I remember my mother saying, "Your grandfather is in prison." I was shocked. *What happened?*

I asked, "Can we go see him?" My mother replied, "No, he is in prison in Cuba."

How could that be? We had just seen him five days prior on Mother's Day.

I had a flashback to Mother's Day. Something was weird. I remember my grandfather giving a speech during Mother's Day to all his grandchildren. It was odd, like a speech you'd make if you were going to die. And now it was apparent why he'd made it. But I was still confused as to why my 73-year-old grandfather and American citizen would be in a Cuban jail.

Photo Credit: Author

The picture my grandfather took with his grandkids on Mother's Day 1998. I'm the guy with the shaved head sitting on the couch on the left.

118

On May 15, 1998, my grandfather, Ernestino Abreu Horta left Key West, Florida in the darkness of the night in a speedboat aimed toward Cuba. The driver of the boat dropped him off several miles off the coast of Cuba. He and his partner hopped onto an inflatable commando boat and stealthily made their way to the coast to meet up with a group connected to the Cuban youth. Their objective was to organize, train, and overthrow the Castro dictatorship.

Over the next few weeks, we started getting more accounts as to what had happened. I recall thinking, *what chance did he have to overthrow the government at 73 years old?* That was crazy to me. What really bothered me was that I didn't have something I believed in so much that it would drive me to attempt the seemingly impossible as my grandfather had done with so much courage and conviction.

Apparently, when my grandfather and his partner landed in Cuba, there was no group

119

waiting to help ensure safe passage. He knew they were in trouble. After several days hiking through the countryside with no food or water, they had to stop at a house for help. Soon after, they were handed over to the authorities. After a few years and lots of petitioning, we brought my grandfather back to the U.S. By his example, I learned the power of having an ironclad vision. My grandfather's vision was that he wanted a free Cuba. He wanted his country back from the communists.

He showed me through his actions, the way he lived his life what it looks like to have a Purpose so powerful you'd be willing to sacrifice your life for it. His home, his land, his family, and his country were taken from him. He was not going out without a fight.

When you discover what you don't want to stop fighting for, you've discovered your Purpose.

CHAPTER 9: THE MUCK REVEALS THE MAGIC

"Life's easy if you live it the hard way, and hard if you live it the easy way."

- Dave Kekich

Growing up, my parents greatly valued education. They knew that earning an education meant getting ahead in life. They immigrated from another country, and in their minds, an education in the U.S. allowed you to move forward. I remember as a kid my father always told me that I was responsible for taking out the trash and cutting the grass. I used to hate it and much preferred playing with my friends, playing sports or video games, and watching TV.

One morning, my dad asked me to take out the trash. I hated taking out the trash. I hated even more that I had to get up early or stop what I was doing to take out the trash. As I was trying to get out of the chore one day, I told my dad, "What's the point of me going to school if all you want me to do are these jobs that don't require education? It doesn't make any sense." Have you ever said something to your parents that as soon as it left your mouth, you knew it was not a good idea? That's how I felt.

It felt as if my 5-foot, 3-inch tall father was towering over me as he looked me square in the eyes and said, "It's not that I want you to become a lawn maintenance guy or that I want you to become a trash man or anything of the sort, but I do want you to be self-reliant. I do want you to value what hard work is all about. If you ever needed a job and had to become a trash man, you could do it. If you ever needed to be a lawn maintenance person, you could do it. It's a skill and a discipline you would have developed, and when you are working under adverse conditions, it builds your character. So, think of this as an education. It's not that this is what I want for you, but the beauty of doing things you don't want to do is that it helps you to narow in on what you do want."

I was blown away. Of course, I still disliked taking out the trash and cutting the lawn, but after my dad explained his rationale, I understood why he needed me to handle my chores. What he said, has stuck with me my whole life.

Too often people try to figure out what is the perfect path in their life. They are trying to solve what they are supposed to be and do. The problem is they sit around thinking about it, and they don't try anything. They lack the focus, the experience, and the context of jobs, careers, or experiences they don't want. They are unsure of what *doesn't* bring happiness or what they *don't* want to do.

Imagine blistering heat, oppressive humidity, hungry bird-sized mosquitoes biting you, and physical labor. Those elements were all part of my summers from 12 to 18 years old working with my dad in construction. He had his own construction company, and I was on the front lines. I carried plywood up and down stairs. I swept and cleaned up the job site because my father always wanted it to look impeccable. I did whatever needed to be done, and I absolutely detested it. Looking back, it was a blessing in disguise because I learned a lot and could spend quality time with my dad. My dad would wake me up at 5 a.m., and we'd go for a run and do calisthenics. Then we'd shower and be at the job site by 6:30 a.m. I learned discipline and the importance of investing in your health first thing in the morning. As I continued to work beside him, I became more proficient in construction work. I can still go to a job site and tell you if things are being done correctly. I learned what it takes to make a living doing that kind of work. It was hard, and very quickly I knew I didn't want to do it when I grew up. Knowing this drove me to study harder and to pursue the areas that did interest me.

Doing the work taught me that through the experience of doing, you gain clarity. I would have never done the work if it weren't for the guidance of my father. This allowed me to make more confident decisions. Too often, I have conversations with men who are still searching for their purpose and how they want to show up in this world. They've never worked those grueling jobs that could help to make it clear what they don't want to do. Even worse, they work at a job they currently hate, but complacency is easier than putting in the work it would take to make a shift.

Perhaps you can relate to being in one of these situations?

If you are feeling confused or uncertain about the path you want to take, the purpose and the mission that you are here for, start doing. Start heading in any direction and using that as data as to whether you want to continue down that path. Ask yourself, *what do I like from here? What am I good at here? What fulfills me here? What brings joy to me? How can I serve others here?*

As you collect your data, you can use it as a reference point to decide what the next step can be or should be for you to move one step closer to your intentions. This is a path of self-discovery and self-discovery is not binary. It is not A or B. It is about revealing a fresh layer that allows you a little bit more clarity, a little bit more certainty, a little bit more confidence and a little bit more excitement as time goes on.

Some people have decided right from the start on what they think they want to do. This was me. I knew from high school I wanted to serve people. At first, I thought I would work with athletes. I knew I wanted my work to revolve around sports performance, and that I wanted to give the best possible service. So, I started with the training component, looking into the performance. I'd ask, "How do I maximize performance?" That led me to study strength and conditioning. Then I started realizing in order to perform optimally you needed to fuel your body precisely. Next, I studied the how to optimize nutrition for performance. Next, I realized that especially at the higher-performing levels as an athlete, you teeter between optimal performance and injury. So, I asked, "How can I help prevent injuries and how can I help athletes recover from them?" My focus progressed naturally into studying athletic training and choosing to do my masters in physical therapy.

As I continued to develop my skills, I worked with more athletes and more and more people. I realized the biggest obstacle or the biggest determinant in success and consistency over time was mindset. I needed to understand the mind more. I needed to understand how people operate and how they do what they do and why they do it. I studied neuroscience, psychology, and the coaching components of how to crack that code in people, so I could better help others transform their mindset. I did this for a few years. Then in 2013, I hit a crossroads where I felt I needed to serve on a deeper level, that the work I was doing could be better, but the problem was I didn't know how to make that happen. It took me into the deep depression. I've shared this story before, but as a result, it almost destroyed my business. I wanted to do something different, and that made me think I had a problem with my business. Often, it's easier to place blame on things than to reflect inside and see where the emptiness or uncertainty lies.

Before you look out, look in. Purpose is an internal driving force. You can find purpose in anything you do. Purpose lives within you. As you read more and go into this deeper and deeper, you will find that it was always there. You just have to remove and remove, and remove all the layers covering it. At first, you see the shadow of it, then the silhouette; and as you keep removing you'll discover more and more detail until at last, you will reveal your masterpiece.

CHAPTER 10: PEOPLE –
ENVIRONMENT BREEDS EXCELLENCE

"A rising tide lifts all boats."

-John F. Kennedy

Your environment is the biggest predictor of your actions and your success. It can be transformative if you learn to leverage it. I felt lucky to have met my coach who shared this with me and now I'm sharing it with you.

This principle allows you to stack the deck in your favor, but you must be deliberate about it. Building and designing an environment that inspires also helps to support you in showing up as the greatest and grandest version of who you are and who you can be.

One of our strongest environmental influences are the people who allow you to be the person you were meant to be. People who support you as you move along, people who help you up when you fall. They are there to encourage you to try again, and when you fail, they still celebrate your progress. Connection with that core group of people makes all the difference.

The right group of people in your life can help you shift your focus from how to survive into how to serve.

Let's explore: think about your friends or family members who understand you, support you and rally behind you. When you are with these people, do you feel like life is dire? Probably not. It's likely just the opposite; being around those people unlocks abundance in your life.

My younger brother was a walk-on Cross Country and Track and Field athlete at Florida State University. Initially, he lacked the discipline to train consistently and step into his potential. Yet, I looked up to him because he is probably one of the most gifted competitors I've seen. His ability to rise to a new level of performance on race day was always inspiring to me. His teammates at FSU were Olympians and national champions. After a year of being surrounded by such high achievers, he started adopting their habits. His performance improved so much that he earned a scholarship and became team captain for his last two years of college.

Photo Credit: Author
My father and I traveled to North Carolina to watch my brother run the Appalachian State Invitational.

The people you surround yourself with and their proximity to you have the power to raise or lower your standards.

We've been trained to focus on things instead of people. Things become a distraction. The very same things that we seek are the very same things that anchor us and slow us down from moving forward, from building the relationships we need to build, and from connecting with the people we love the most in our lives.

There are three different circles of people I want you to think about as you read this next section.

Photo Credit: mhiz_wendy

First and foremost is your inner circle, your core group of people. These people will amplify or suppress the best version of you. You've probably heard the saying that "You're the average of the five people you spend the most time with." That means financially and creatively, as well as how they affect your generosity, focus, and goals; you become the average of those five people. Your environment and the people who you surround yourself with have massive amounts of influence on you. They influence how you think, what you do, what you say, and how you live. So, having the right core group of people, your High 5 crew, is vital. Your High 5 Crew is the people who help nurture and protect your vision and your purpose, as you are developing them.

Think about and write down the 5 people in your life that you spend the most time with? This could be family, a best friend, or work colleague. They could be authors or people you watch on TV or listen to their podcasts everyday—meaning these people are feeding your brain/soul daily. They are indirectly shaping you even though you don't necessarily spend time with them in person.

Most of us end up with our High 5 Crew because of proximity and convenience. Is your current High 5 Crew aligned with your values? Are they aligned with your vision? Do they demand excellence from you? It's vital that you purposefully surround yourself with your High 5 Crew. You can have more than five, or you can have less, but five seems to be statistically the number that is just right for exponential growth.

The second circle of people are the people who matter most in your life. I'm sure you're asking, "Why are they not in the first circle?" The distinction is that in your High 5 Crew you actively choose them because they help you show up as the best version of yourself. The people that matter most very often drive your purpose, like your wife, kids, and family. People in your second circle could be part of your High 5 Crew and vice versa. I consider my wife as one of the most important members in my High 5 Crew and she is also one of the people that matters most in my life.

For the people that matter most:

- How do your daily actions allow those that matter most in your life to know how much they mean to you?
- How are you serving and supporting them daily?
- How are you present in their lives?

Answering these questions can bring you greater understanding as to if you are really serving them to your potential.

The third circle is made up of the people you serve. I believe that we've been put on this earth to serve others. Our society says, "We are here for ourselves. Do only what makes you happy and tell everyone else to f*@K off!" This is the recipe for unhappiness and being unfulfilled. There is something greater than ourselves and when we step up to serve others it helps bring out the best in others and ourselves.

I believe purpose without people is pointless. Purpose without people is void. It's void of significance, void of joy, and void of drive. You must nurture people and cultivate relationships to continue to grow as the best version of you. Your relationships can't become static. In fact, once they become static, you cease to grow, and that relationship starts withering away. We see it often with families, marriages, and friendships. What we do, what we say, who we are being, it all becomes food to nourish those relationships. How we communicate helps to inspire that purpose, that drive.

One day I was running with my wife and we were talking about each other's strengths. She really fed my soul when she shared how she's observed me take my immersive personality to be used to help others and be extremely consistent with my daily routines. Her acknowledging that was a big deal for me as well as for our relationship.

I hear stories of fathers who are overweight, who are sedentary, who haven't done anything in their life until finally they are overcome with fear. They realize they may not be around for their kids. They realize they might not be around to experience their kid's first steps, their first day of school, their graduation, their first date, their wedding day, or their grandkids. They face a very stark reality: either they continue down their current path and miss the lives of their children, or they turn 180 degrees, because their child, wife, and future grandchildren are worthy of sticking around for.

When they make that change, what they have made is a commitment. They have made a declaration they are worthy to live optimally and to be in the lives of their family. The problem is that circumstances aren't always so black and white. When we meet with that bone-chilling contrast, where it's life or death, often, it's easier to make that decision. Then life comes into focus. But what happens when life becomes insidious? What happens when the grays creep into our life? What happens when average becomes the norm? What happens when there is a small leak and it slowly starts to empty you?

We have an epidemic of men facing a future with their life, energy, and purpose drained from them. If you feel this way, is it still acceptable for you to live your life in the manner you are living it? I am not judging you when I ask this question. It's something you need to ask yourself as you look in the mirror to decide if you want to or need to make a change.

Is average okay with you?

Is just getting by okay?

It is your choice. It is a decision you need to make. It is one you will have to live with, and you will have to live with the consequences as well.

When I was growing up, my father and I had conversations about these very topics. The two places I remember having the bulk of these conversations were during our many training sessions and in the car. We ran, cycled, skated, or lifted daily for hours and took those opportunities to talk about everything. We also discussed life and these deep thoughts on road trips and during regular commutes. During one of our trips to North Carolina, we talked the entire 14-hour drive to the point where I had a sore throat the next day.

I remember specifically my father telling me about the consequences of the choices each of us makes. It's not about good or bad; it is about understanding that every choice, every action you take has a consequence. When you are clear on your values, your vision, and your purpose, you can look at those consequences and decide if they are acting in alignment with what you want, and you can take a stand.

Writing is not one of my gifts; it is very difficult for me. So, why write a book if I am not a writer? Because it's not about writing a book. I didn't decide to write a book to become an author. I am writing this book because this message is greater than me. This message is more important to me than any difficulty or struggle I have to go through to write it. There have been plenty of difficulties, struggles, and obstacles to get this book done. Even though it's challenging for me to write, what is interesting is that going through the fire, and struggle and coming out on the other end is liberating. It strengthens my character. It reaffirms why my message is so important, that I'd be willing to go and do and get uncomfortable over it. That's the meaning of purpose. It is something that drives you into the face of discomfort and the face of obstacles. It is that internal push allowing you to persevere even in dire and uncomfortable circumstances.

Keep those people who matter most around you. They will help you put things in perspective. There have been studies published and books written of successful men and women on their death beds and none of them ever had the regret of wishing they'd worked more. None. Much the opposite—pretty much all of them said they'd wished they hadn't worked so much, that they'd have spent more time with their family, the people who matter most. The choice is yours.

Don't be afraid to be honest with yourself. Know what you want and create it. Surround yourself with those people that love you, uplift you, support you, and challenge you. Finally, serve others with purpose and intent.

SECTION 4 – YOUR PROCESS

CHAPTER 11: INNOVATION, SERVICE, AND CONTRIBUTION

"Exploration is the engine that drives innovation. Innovation drives economic growth. So, let's all go exploring."

– Edith Widder

Process is how you go about creating your legacy. The how is often where most people get caught up because they forget to do the work you just did to get clear on your Vision (what) and on your Purpose (why).

Three amplifiers of process are innovation, service, and contribution.

To innovate is to create something that wasn't there before, to do something in a way that's never been done, to structure in a way that releases the brakes from the impossible.

Innovation transforms lives, communities, industries, and time. In periods where innovations flourish, we see massive leaps in how people think, live and operate. When you are clear about your purpose, that purpose gets amplified through innovation. You can only execute innovation when you are clear about your purpose and clear on the next steps you want to take.

One of the greatest innovators was Leonardo da Vinci. They called him a Renaissance Man. Renaissance means re-birth, and he was the embodiment of that. He was an author, painter, sculptor, and inventor. He was pretty much anything and everything. He innovated in mechanics, anatomy and physiology as well as in art. He seemed to have mastered his left and right brain; the analytical and the creative. He bridged the gap between both worlds and as a result pushed an era forward.

Da Vinci had a strong and distilled vision and a driving purpose that allowed him to carry on after many failures. Most men celebrate their successes but few realize that it was through the insights of their failure that they were able to succeed. The problem with us men is that all we see are the successes of others. Rarely do we see all the failures and tribulations that allowed someone else to succeed. It is easy to think that you can succeed until you are met with failure. This can be humbling as you proceed, expecting success to occur linearly without any failures. Just remember, you didn't see that closet full of failures they had to go through to get to their success. Embrace your journey. Don't compare it to those before you.

Thomas Edison said he'd figured out 1,000 ways how not to make a lightbulb until eventually, he figured out how to make the light bulb.

Would you have the persistence to fail 1000 times?

Would your purpose be strong enough to endure 1,000 failures before you finally figured it out—because it was so important to you?

Would your reason why drive you past all the failures?

Service heightens your purpose. Man is not an island. We are mammals. We were designed to be a community, not hermits. One of the biggest disservices you can do both to yourself and to your community is to think about you and you alone. This mindset is one of the biggest signs of insecurity. By insecurity I mean that you become afraid of helping others because they may get ahead of you or be better than you. It is a sign you lack clarity in your purpose.

When you are clear on your purpose, what you find is that service only amplifies it. One of my favorite quotes by Abraham Lincoln is "No man is so tall as when he stoops down to help a child (or someone in need.)" Think about the times when you were beaten to the floor by life, by circumstances or by struggles. Maybe somebody lent you a helping hand. How did that feel? I've been on the receiving end many times. I can tell you it is transformative. It is uplifting. It is getting the gift of hope.

What I know to be true is that helping someone else will bring more love and certainty into your life. It will bring more comfort to you. It brings more joy, which puts you in a better place to accept more clarity. For the other person, it could mean the difference between life and death. Service is powerful. I believe being self-reliant is important. But I also believe that serving others and accepting help from others can help shift us from surviving to thriving. I love the African proverb that says, "If you want to go fast, go alone. If you want to go far, go together."

When you come with a heart of abundance it is infinitely easier to give to others no matter your situation. Abundance is infinite; it's a mindset. It's a way of looking and interacting with others, with this world. Abundance doesn't come from having lots of money or things. Abundance is a way of being that brings out the best version of who you are being. Part of abundance is to be humble and open to receive. This is probably one of the most difficult things for us men to do. To receive is to put our ego and pride aside. To receive help, to receive compliments, to receive perspective, to receive love, this is a part of service, too. Service is not only about giving but also about receiving graciously.

Another key component of process is contribution. It is part of living in abundance. Contribution can be giving of your gifts, talents, financial support, and/or your time.

For a long time, I'd ignore homeless people because I didn't want to give them money. Sometimes because I didn't have cash and felt embarrassed I couldn't help and other times because I started judging them without even knowing their situation.

Think back to the last time you were in your car and a homeless person asked for money. What were your thoughts?

Then I had kids. Kids have a way of bringing perspective to a situation. Currently, they are eight, six, and three years old and they don't ignore the homeless people. They'd ask questions about why they were homeless or why we weren't helping them. I didn't have a good answer. In fact, I was embarrassed. My actions were unacceptable to me. I want my kids to be compassionate, empathetic and my actions were not expressing that. The kids and I decided to make zip lock bags filled with cards the kids made, snacks, water, and tissues.

The next time we saw a homeless man I rolled down the window and gave it to him. I smiled and felt good. Then the kids asked, "What was his name?" I was stumped. I had no idea, I never asked.

Sure, I had helped a homeless man by giving him some food but it was a transaction. I missed the most important part, actually connecting with him. I told the kids that next time we saw the man I'd ask his name. Sure enough two days later on the way back from picking the kids up from school there he was. Once again, we gave him one of our gift bags. I asked, "Hi my name is

Armando, what's your name?" He looked a little shocked. He said, "Tom." "It's a pleasure to meet you, Tom. I hope this helps some," I replied. He very gratefully thanked us as we left.

Here is what that experience taught me. The most important thing I could have given Tom was not my money, food, or clothes, it was acknowledgement. Tom and many homeless people spend days, months and years being ignored. We have everything we need right now to abundantly serve others. As we'd see Tom on our way back from school, I'd stop, look him in the eyes, shake his hand and the kids would say hi to Tom.

There is a South African greeting from the Zulu tribe, "Sawubona" that means: "I see you." I believe one of the greatest gifts or contributions you can give to others is to truly see them. See them without judgment but for who they are.

How can you give the best of you in your health, faith, relationships, and experiences to make your community and the world a better place?

CHAPTER 12: ONE DROP AT A TIME

"Success is not the absence of failure; it's the persistence through failure."

- Aisha Tyler

A drop of water seems insignificant. By itself it is. If a faucet drips once per second by the end of a year, it will fill 347 gallon jugs in a year. Talk about a hell of a water bill. To give you context of what that would look like, if you stacked 347 1-gallon milk jugs on top of each other it would be the height of a 30-story building. The brutal Chinese water torture consisted of a drop of water landing on the forehead of a prisoner who was tied down for days and weeks. It is not the first drop that had an effect but the consistency of drop after drop that delivered a sledgehammer blow to the head.

The most powerful actions are often missed because they seem so ordinary and when done once, have little impact. It is the accumulation over time that amplifies their impact.

What actions do you perform daily that align with your values, to help you create that vision you described earlier? Knowing the answer to this question is vital to living your purposeful and powerful legacy. Executing actions that align with your values will help you leave the legacy that excites you and inspires you, that leaves the mark you are capable of, the one you want to bequeath to this world for the people who matter the most in your life.

Earlier in this book, we spoke about the importance of values, and I shared with you the value system I created that is part of the R.I.C.H. Man Experience.

Your values act not as an anchor you drag, but as a compass to guide you, as a propeller to move you forward. Your value system must be nimble and agile to quickly and accurately assist you in every decision you make. Your values allow you to definitively and concretely recognize the actions and steps you need to take to move in the direction you want.

Not all actions are created equally. Consider the actions that matter most to you. Consider the actions that take the least resistance for you to start, that will allow you the most consistency. An action done once doesn't provide the compounding interest that daily actions provide.

Let's travel back in time to an example I shared previously in this book to answer the following question: *"How do I know I am showing up as the best man that I can be?"*

My clients and I use the R.I.C.H. Man value system. I'd encourage you to do the same. But if you decide to create your own, keep in mind it must be functional, and to be functional, it must be truthful, agile, and flexible. Truthful, in that, you must believe in what you set forth. You must be clear on how exactly you define your values and that they fit your beliefs. Agile means they must allow you to quickly and accurately course-correct your direction at a moment's notice. Life will bring about many unknowns, and you must be agile for this reason. Being flexible gives you the ability to travel light. You will move and feel differently. It is the difference between carrying 10 pounds on your shoulders versus 100 pounds. Using a nimble value system frees up more energy and gives you the tools needed to assess the action needed accurately.

Go back to the question, "*How do I know I am showing up as the best man that I can be,*" and answer it using the R.I.C.H. Man value system.

Let's say you are at work and one of your employees or one of the people you manage drops the ball on something important. How do you show up in that situation?

Ask yourself, am I being or showing up as a man who is respected? What does a respected man look like, sound like, and act like? My definition of a respected man is that he has compassion and keeps his composure. He is in control of the situation and his emotions. He is effective and efficient. A respected man is truthful and honest.

Ask, *am I showing up from a place of inspiration or am I coming from a place of need?* An inspired man doesn't lash out in anger because he is disappointed in someone. An inspired man shines a light where there is darkness. An inspired man can see what others can't. He can distinguish what is most important.

Ask, *am I truly connected to myself and honestly showing up presently and powerfully?* A connected man is sure of himself and doesn't have to put others down to feel better about himself. He is confident and accepts himself for who he is and embraces it. Ask, *am I genuinely connecting with my employee?* A connected man actively listens to better understand differing points of view and how to best address them.

Ask, *am I coming from a place of happiness and joy?* A happy man chooses to view the world through a lens of abundance and joy. Perhaps in this opportunity, the lens of happiness is to serve your employee and empower him to show up as a R.I.C.H. Man.

The R.I.C.H. Man value system will help guide you and shape your daily actions similar to that drop of water. There will be some roadblocks, obstacles, pitfalls, and struggles. As men, we have been told to "just man up" or "just do it." That is not what I am talking about. This is not my saying, "Hey, just man up and do it. If you were a real man, you'd just get it done and not complain about it or give excuses." There is enough of that mentality already. In some instances, yes, you would do that. But why not give yourself the benefit of the doubt and honestly explore where you actually are? You'd be surprised to find walking through doors is easier, more enjoyable, and leaves you with more energy than trying to break through walls all the time.

The "just do it" mentality is a byproduct of not being as skillful in one area as you are in another. When I went to work in construction with my dad, we had to move lots of heavy material and tools around. My first tendency was to lift everything and just grind it out. My father, who is an engineer, taught me to use levers, pulleys, and wheels to move things with significantly less effort and fewer chances for injury. I remember transporting a machine weighing over 800 pounds. My initial thought was, *"How are we going to get enough people to load this on the van?"* I did the math and knew that no matter how much my dad and I had been working out we were definitely not lifting an awkward machine 3-4 feet off the ground to load it into the van if it weighed that much.

My father had a different idea. We put it on wheels, made a ramp, and used pulleys and a ratchet system to slowly and carefully load the monster machine into the van. I wanted to lift it (no skill); my father had knowledge of physics (i.e., skill) that allowed him to load the machine safely, effectively, and efficiently.

Let's say my dad and I mustered up the strength to lift the machine. How long do you think we would have been able to continue doing that before we got hurt? Using my dad's approach of utilizing the skills and applications of physics allowed us to lift that machine for a longer time. More skill equals long-term sustainable results with less effort.

In all honesty, it may be difficult for you to self-assess and that's where the help of a coach comes in. That's where working with someone with an outside perspective who has your best interests in mind serves you better. I share the following with my clients: "You can't see the picture when you're in the frame." Sometimes those roadblocks, those struggles, those pitfalls that you encounter time and time again are there because you don't even see them. You don't see them coming. In my case, working with my coaches over the years has given me the direction I needed to get through the roadblocks and patterns that continued to stop me.

I feel blessed I get to do that same work specifically with growth minded men like you that want to show up more powerfully in their relationships, health, business and contribution to create a purposeful and powerful legacy.

I am sure at some point in your life you've had a conversation with a buddy who was struggling with something or stressing about something and couldn't figure out what to do. Once he shared his struggle with you, it became clear what he needed to do. You had the gift of perspective that he couldn't see.

Let's go back to the vision you created when you wrote out your eulogy. Get super clear on what that vision is and how you can begin to take the steps to break it down. You can work backward and say, "If this is who I want to become, what I want to achieve and how I would like to impact people, what does that look like on a yearly, monthly, weekly, daily, and hourly basis?"

Writing this book encompasses one of the action steps I am taking to create the impact I want to have on others. Part of my legacy I consciously and purposely work toward is impacting the lives of as many men as I can. I want to positively impact the lives of as many families as I can. I want to help build more connected and empowered communities. I want to change the world to think and act in abundance and love.

When I wrote my eulogy from the perspective of my son, part of what I wrote was meant to let my kids know what it means to be a man, and a husband, and how to serve your wife. It was to instill in them the habits of a producer, instead of a consumer. I wanted to ensure my son knew the meaning of impacting the lives of others.

As I reflected on that eulogy, one of the things that became apparent to me was that it is important for me to share my message, my beliefs, and my thoughts with the world. I feel it is part of my calling and purpose to celebrate and share the valuable insights and influences I gained through watching and talking with my father. I'm inspired to share the clarity I recognized as it relates to my experiences and studies: the good, the bad, and the ugly. I wanted to share all those stories and insights in this book because I know there are men just like you and me who will benefit from these experiences.

This book contains the kind of insight I wish I'd had when I was struggling. Writing this book was a test of my values. *Do I just write what is easy and what everyone wants to hear?* I had to align with my R.I.C.H. Man values of Respected, Inspired, Connected, and Happy. But to do that, I had to make the creation of this book mean something that would make me feel connected, that would make me feel inspired, that would make me feel happy. I needed to write a message that I could respect. I focused on everything I enjoyed about the writing process. The things that did not inspire me like the editing, formatting, and all the tech stuff, I outsourced. That freed me up to concentrate on the creating part. I love to create. I was creating the concept, the message, the structure, and the book itself. This book contributes to the impact I'd like to have on others, and how it affects my overall legacy.

How do you want to feel in your process?

How can you align the values of Respected, Inspired, Connected and Happy to ensure you are congruent with your process?

Too often we think we are too busy, the time is not right, but there is no time like right now. Tomorrow is promised to no one.

I am sure you have heard of the scenario if today was your last day on earth what would you do? Would you do anything different? Would you do everything the same? What if you knew you had a week to live, a month to live, how would you live each and every day? I venture to say if you knew with that much certainty you had such little time left, you would probably focus on spending time with the people who matter most in your life. You'd spend time immersed in experiences that fulfill you. You'd make sure not to waste time. In answering the questions above, what I realized is that there are a few key components in my life. Perhaps you can borrow them, or maybe they can give you some insights as to a few of the things you can focus on.

If I knew that I was going to die in one month, or even a week, or even a day, there are certain things that I would like to have done on a day-to-day basis.

I've found that spending time with people who matter most, doing something that inspires me or excites me, growing and learning daily as well as doing something to serve others are the main things I would do.

You see, growth is a big component of fulfillment. If you are not growing every day, the likelihood of feeling fulfilled is minimal. It's part of our human need.

So, now, I would ask you to take yourself through the same exercise. Just imagine you are living a Groundhog Day, where every day would be the same, or you knew in one month, you were going to die. What non-negotiable components would become a part of your day-to-day life?

CHAPTER 13: NOT WORK/LIFE BALANCE – JUST LIFE

"The challenge of work/life balance is without question one of the most significant struggles faced by modern man."

– Stephen Covey

You don't want balance. One of the biggest distractions we face as men is this idea of work/life balance. In my opinion, work/life balance as a theory to believe in sets you up for failure and is not a framework that will serve you and your family well.

Before I go more in-depth on that topic, let me give you a definition of work/life balance, and then I'll invite you to try on a different framework to see what serves you best.

What is work life balance?

As most men think about it, work/life balance is the idea that you should spend equal time, energy, and effort at home as you spend at work.

We hear the media, authors, and leaders talk about it all the time and as men, it's probably one of the things we very often get wrong. In interviewing these successful and insightful men for this book what I found is that everyone had an idea on this, and I think there are a lot of misunderstandings concerning work/life balance. As I mentioned above, work/life balance is the concept of spending the same amount of time with your family, on your health, in your work and in your business, as well as on all the concerns that matter to you. If all of those things balance out, then you have work/life balance.

But what if I told you that work/life balance was not what you really wanted. The idea that you want balance is a very nice one that we've been led to believe is the ultimate solution, but the fact is, what you want is imbalance. You want movement. You want growth. You want progress.

Let me say that again, "What you want is imbalance!"

Think about a see-saw.

What happens if you are balanced on a seesaw? There is no movement. You have the same amount of weight on both sides. No ups and downs means no fun. Let me share a different analogy.

Have you ever seen the graph of an EKG?

An electrocardiogram or EKG is a test that checks for electrical problems in your heart. A healthy heart displays the peaks above the baseline and the valleys below the baseline. When people shoot for balance, they are shooting to live on the baseline without any peaks and valleys. Medically speaking, it means you've flat lined—that you are dead!

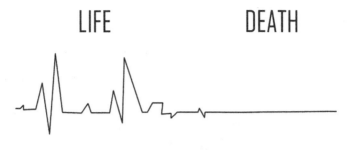

EMBRACE LIFE'S UPS & DOWNS!

Photo Credit: mhiz_Wendy

Let's try a different analogy. Think about the context of running. One of my coaches referred to running as "controlled falling". If you think about that for a second, it makes sense. If you're trying to go from point A to point B, the last thing you want is to be balanced because, when you are balanced you are not moving. Strive instead, for controlled falling to get you moving in the direction you want to go.

When Christian and I got married, it was hard in the beginning. She kept telling me she didn't feel loved. That was tough to hear. I told her daily that I loved her. I hugged and kissed her all the time. How could she think I didn't love her? I finally asked her (duh) what would make her feel loved? Her response was, "Spend more quality time with me."

I was confused. "What do you mean?"

She said, "We spend time in the same space together but that's not quality time, it's just time. Quality time is when you are focused on me and not distracted by other things. It is when we get to talk and connect."

I've said it before. Context is crucial. If I hadn't asked Christian what would make her feel loved, I would have continued doing what I was doing, and she would have continued feeling unloved. It's not the quantity of time you spend with someone but the quality of your time with them. The same rings true for this idea of work/life balance. It is all about being present and making the most of the time you do have.

Let's take the average eight-hour workday. Add at least an extra hour to that since the average commute time is about 26 minutes each way according to the U.S. Census Bureau. To achieve work/life balance in the traditional sense, we would have to spend an equal amount of time with the family. If we did the math, you'd find we are already 18 hours into the day, which only leaves six hours to sleep, exercise, and do anything else you want. It is not that this schedule couldn't happen, but it may not be what you want, or what would serve you and your family best.

I encourage you to pay attention to the quality of time you spend with people. How present are you in each situation? There are different seasons in your life and different times and ways to invest in your life and your family's life. For instance, when you are with the family on vacation, are you present? Are you there mentally? If you are off distracted by work, then that's a different reality than the one for which we're striving.

I've been in that situation. I have to remind myself of my true purpose for being in that moment as I create boundaries to ensure I am present. During the summer, Friday is family beach day. My wife and I schedule any clients early in the morning then we arrive at the beach at noon and stay until 7pm. We spend the day talking and enjoying nature. It's one of the times that we really enjoy. We have our secret secluded spot. The kids just play in the sand and surf all day. If you are going on vacation then be present there. Enjoy the experience. On the other hand, if you are launching a new business or product, you need to channel an initial investment of time, energy and focus toward these ventures to give them a chance to succeed. Some people aren't willing to sacrifice that time while others set a time-limit boundary, and do not cross it.

Ask yourself, "Is spending this time, taking on this new project and doing these things worth it at the expense of my family?" Because there is a limited amount of time in the day. You only have a specific amount of energy and focus. As such, you must make sure you are deliberate in the way you use it. So, again, is this something you need to be doing? If no, then don't do it. If yes, then ask how do I ensure that this aligns with my values?

I interviewed a friend of mine, Connor Beaton, the founder of ManTalks. One of the things he said, which I think is a wonderful way to look at work/life balance is to really *not* look at work/life balance, per se. Instead, examine your life under the lens of priority management.

What are your priorities for the day? How can you maximize your time, your focus, and your energy on those priorities? Your actions illustrate your priorities. One of the things I share with my clients is, "Where your actions lay is a strong indication of where your priorities lay."

Think about this for a second.

Where do your actions and thus priorities lie? You can say my family is the most important thing to me, but are they if you're never around? If you are never actually with them, then you are not developing a relationship with them. Or, you can say your health is your priority but is it if you eat junk, never exercise, never sleep, and don't drink water? Is your health a priority if you smoke and drink too much? You can say, you can list, you can plan your priorities but at the end of the day, your actions will say what your priorities are and will ultimately create the legacy you leave. Therefore, part of showing up as an authentic man is being true to your word and aligning your actions with your values and beliefs, your vision, and your purpose. Align your actions with your priorities—the priorities you want to have so you can live the legacy you want to leave.

What do you have to do to align with your vision, your purpose, and your process?

When you feel off-track, ask yourself that

question and dissect those areas of your life. If you start looking out before you look in, you'll miss the boat. The frustration comes when you lack the clarity and patience because you have started looking for shortcuts to get there quicker. The end result is a weak foundation to work on and from which to build.

My oldest son was four when he said, "You always say we will play later but later never comes and then it is time for bed." My heart sank. I worked mostly from home so he'd come in the office throughout the day and ask to play with me. I'd say, "Later, I need to finish my work." By the time I'd finish it would be his bedtime and we wouldn't get to play.

That conversation made me evaluate the way I worked. Was I actually being productive or was I being busy? I had to look in and really decide what was most important for me. What I found was being an awesome father is one of the most important things I could aspire to be. I changed things up. Whenever he asked to play we'd set a timer for 10 minutes. We'd play then I'd go back to work and set a work timer for 40 minutes. As a result, I got to spend more time with my son playing plus I actually got more important work done because I was hyper-focused for 40 minutes.

Let's take a step back for a second.

Work/Life balance is not what you need. Balance causes stagnation. You want movement that aligns with your vision, purpose, and process. Prioritize your actions by scheduling them into your day first.

I remember living with constant guilt and frustration when I could not find satisfaction in how I was spending my time. When I was at work, I felt I had to be with my family; when I was with my family, I felt like I should work on and grow my business. It was making me miserable and it didn't allow me to show up to any one of these responsibilities well. I always felt I needed to be somewhere else.

Have you ever felt guilty when you were with the family because you felt like you should be at work or vice-versa?

The reason for my guilt was due to a lack of clarity. I constantly heard I needed to catch this unicorn called "work/life balance."

I mentioned earlier, that focusing on priority management instead of work/life balance was a really helpful way to create a practical process to improve my outcome.

Ask yourself, *what are my priorities and do my actions support my priorities?*

When I focused on the important areas in my life, my path became clear. My health, my family, my faith, my business, and my impact, were my priorities. Once I identified my priorities, I scheduled them in my calendar and set up a supportive environment to ensure I get them done.

The first thing I had to do was get vitally clear on exactly what my priorities were. You can imagine what it's like going to work thinking you should be at home or going home and always feeling you should be at work.

How frustrating and unsatisfying is that?

Once I had clarity in my priorities and they aligned with my vision, and purpose, I could create a process that supports it. I started scheduling time and space to experience and nurture my priorities. This created a different experience. I no longer felt I needed to be elsewhere.

Gaining that level of clarity will bring peace to your life. Think about this for a moment. You're in the right place at the right time because you created the space for it.

- How can you create space for the life you want?
- How can you create the space to do the work that inspires you?
- How can you create the space to revitalize your health?
- How can you create the space to create the relationship you want with your wife and kids?
- How can you create the space to leave the impact or the contribution you want to leave in this world?

You see, if you don't create that space and time for your priorities, the likelihood of you investing the time and energy needed to live them out diminishes significantly. If you don't schedule it, there is a good chance you may be distracted when you're trying to be present because a shining object somewhere else is drawing you, and you are focusing your attention on that distraction instead of what you need to be doing. Create the space today.

Let me share with you my Big 3 System that will improve your consistency for effectively and efficiently spending your time on your priorities.

Step 1: Schedule your personal and family time. That means your exercise, mediation, reading, learning or whatever "me" time you want and need. Then schedule out non-negotiable family time.

Step 2: Write out the 3 most important things you must get done the following day. Schedule the time to do them.

Step 3: Schedule the other stuff. The other work stuff, meetings, errands, etc...

Whenever you hear "work/life balance," don't think of it in the traditional sense, as if the same number of hours needs to be allocated for work and home. Focus on your priorities.

When I decided to write this book, I was running my fitness and physical therapy studio, my Legacy coaching business, and putting together my first Modern Man Virtual Summit, where I video-interviewed 20 different experts, authors, and coaches from all over the world to create a platform where men can learn from these experts to show up more powerfully in their life and work as well as to grow their relationships with their wife and kids.

In the midst of all this, I was committed to putting in the work to write this book in such a way that it would transform the lives of those who read it. I decided to crowd source different perspectives from men in different stages of life. I invested several hours a week interviewing these men. In fact, I interviewed 111 men in a span of 37 days.

I remembered knowing consciously that I wasn't going to be able to spend the time that I would love to spend with my kids, yet sharing this message is part of my Impact Legacy.

It was late in the evening. My kids were ready for bed in their pajamas, and I sat them down on the couch. I had a conversation with my 8-year-old, my 5-year-old and my 2-year-old. I told them, "Daddy is writing a book and putting on a conference that will help other men and other dads create better lives for them and their families." I continued, "You know how much fun we have on adventures or when we play games together?" They said, "Yes." "Do you think other kids would like to do those kinds of things with their dad?" I asked them. They said, "Yes!" I told them in order for me to help these dads, it meant I was going to be working more and leaving at different times than they were used to. I told them I'd be on the phone a lot more so I could interview other dads and get to know them better.

In the past, I would have had a significant

internal struggle with this project. Investing all my time away from my family to do something that wasn't guaranteed would have worn on me. This time was different. Once I made up my mind on what I wanted to do and why it was important, it felt as if I was set free to do it. I believe the reason this felt so different was because I got very clear on my vision (provide a blueprint for men to purposely and powerfully create a legacy that inspires and excites them), my purpose (to help men show up more powerfully and purposefully in their health, relationships, business, adventure, and purpose so that they can have more fulfilling marriages, be more present for their kids and have a greater impact on the world), and my process (to write a book, create a virtual summit, and provide legacy coaching and immersive adventures to guide men through this process.)

I asked the kids, "Are you guys okay with that? Can you see why this is important? Do you have any questions?" Their big question was: "Are we still going to go on adventures with you?" "Of course," I replied. Once they were satisfied, they were excited about the plan. This helped, because when I had to leave for work to do the interviews, they knew why. It wasn't that I was abandoning them or that I wasn't paying attention to them. It was, *Daddy is doing this, and I know why he's doing it. I understand why it's important.* Don't get me wrong; I scheduled time with them, even if it was less time than we were used to.

The lesson to take away here is the importance of setting up agreements beforehand. Give your family and your inner circle clarity, and once you do, you will find instead of your absence becoming a contention for separation and an obstacle for the people in your life who matter most, the new routine or the changes in your life become an opportunity to rally around a cause.

During the same time, all this was going on I was training to run a 50-mile race in the Everglades swamps. Yes, 50 miles in one day running through the swamps, so my training also took time. To prepare, I had to put in the hours running.

How was I able to juggle this?

I had to review my vision, purpose and priorities and see how this new aim aligned with these. I wanted to spend time with my wife, so I scheduled it. I wanted to spend time with my kids, so I scheduled it. I had to spend time writing this book, and I scheduled it. I needed to interview guys for the summit and the book and scheduled that time as well. Finally, I needed to run my regular business—my fitness and physical therapy studio. I took all those priorities and factored them in to fit in the training, while not disrupting everything else. I did most of my runs at 3 or 4 a.m. when everyone else was sleeping. I learned you are going to go through times when you will concentrate in one area more than you will invest in other areas. Make sure you stay aligned with your values, vision, and purpose and then create a process that supports your priorities for each day and season of your life.

SECTION 5 –

IMPLEMENTATION

CHAPTER 14: SIMPLICITY & CONSISTENCY – THE WINNING FORMULA

"In character, in manner, in style, in all things, the supreme excellence is simplicity."

- Henry Wadsworth Longfellow

You are going to die. That is a certainty. Everyone you know is going to die. I'm not being negative but sharing the inevitable. You don't get to decide when you are born, and most of us will never know when we will die, but all of us have each day to make the most of our lives.

Your self-improvement, growth, and legacy don't ever stop until you are gone. You may be asking yourself, *what do I do now?* After clarifying your vision, understanding your purpose, and crafting your process, it is time to implement.

If you want to have long-term success in living your legacy, then you need to create an environment where you'll have a win-win situation, where you'll have simple daily rituals that will allow you to be consistent.

Let's be clear. Life is about playing the long game. You only stop when you're dead. As a result, self-improvement, growth, and legacy shouldn't stop until you are gone. In order for this to happen keep things simple so you can be consistent.

The Massive Action Paradox

You have probably heard the phrase, "You have to take massive action."

But what does massive action mean?

The truth is that "massive action" is one of those phrases like "taking it to the next level," or "crushing it," or "game changer," what I call puffery statements. They give no precise direction, path or destination. They are full of hot air. They have become part of our communication as a society, as entrepreneurs, and as men, but they do us a big disservice when we want to clearly and confidently move forward because they are too general.

Precision is a sign of clarity.

These puffery statements imply you are doing something big and grand, but the reality is they become a hiding place for those without clarity. To create an action plan for yourself and to execute it on a consistent level, you must define it. You must be very clear on exactly the type of action you will take. You need to create the kind of action designed to endure.

While taking massive action can be a tool to help propel or shock you out of your current state, in the long term it can be an inefficient and unsustainable practice. Instead, you must have a sustainable long-term strategy to continue progressing in the direction you desire. Consider the space shuttle; it burns through most of the fuel to break through the earth's gravitational pull. Once it is in space, it uses minimal fuel to maneuver because there is no more gravity and resistance slowing it down. When you are starting out, you may need to take that massive action to get you out of your funk or current state. This will demand a big effort of focus and commitment.

As you move into your flow, just like when you are in outer space there won't be that gravity, that resistance slowing you down. You'll focus on the long–term daily strategies, and that will get you where you want to go efficiently and effectively.

Your legacy is created over the years, months, weeks, days, hours, and minutes in which you live your life. When talking about your Personal Legacy, it's the relationships that you continue to build and grow on a day-to-day basis. Your Impact Legacy is better related to innovation, service, or contribution that helped move a society forward, like Thomas Edision's light bulb. You are trying to cultivate an impression with staying power that will make a ripple effect for you, and for the people who come after you.

The first time I ran a 50-mile race, I did it on a whim. I had been saying for years I wanted to run a 50-mile race. I would declare I was going to train for it year after year, but then something would come up. I would get injured. I wouldn't train for it, and time kept passing. Then one year, I saw a post for the Everglades 50 Milers, which is a trail race in the swamps of the Florida Everglades. It happened to fall on the day before my birthday. I decided if I was going to break the cycle of not following through on my declarations, I had to take a big leap of faith and take massive action. I registered three weeks before the race.

The most I had been running consistently at that time was three times a week for about 30 minutes at a time. The longest run I had done then was 90 minutes. I had competed at the collegiate level, and after college, continued to train hard for several years but that was many years ago, and I was no longer a competitive runner.

I remember thinking at that moment, "*I am going to sign up for it and see what happens*". I needed to break my pattern of waiting for the perfect time. The perfect time was not coming, ever. So, I just did it. I took massive action. I registered as I thought, *"what's the worst that could happen? I walk, feel pain, and at the very least it would seem like I was at Disney World."* You know how you can walk all day if you are in Disney World. That was the mentality I used to frame that race.

I had not trained to run 50 miles. I knew if I wanted to succeed I had to go slow, relax, enjoy the show, and see what happened. On race day, I stood nervously by myself. Of course, I was unprepared.

Have you ever felt unprepared for a situation that you've put yourself in or one that life gifted to you?

Standing on the start line I recall telling myself, *make sure you relax, make sure you go slow, slow, slow.* As soon as the gun went off, I found myself in the front with the top seven runners. We were cruising down a dirt road with only our headlamps to reveal the road a few feet in front of us. After four miles, the sun started to rise just as we stepped onto lush, green, single-track trails— the swampland surrounding us. Wild orange trees scattered throughout the swamp were remnants of Indian inhabitants who had lived there. We passed these curious structures and kept pounding the road. After 10 miles, I felt good and thought I could win the race.

Time out.

Do you remember how I started this story? No training, first ever 50-mile race, and I had the delusion to think I could win after only 10 miles.

Time in; let's get back to the story.

I decided to pick up the pace and leave everyone behind. I felt as if I were being hunted as I ran for my life through the overgrown trail, looking back to see if whatever was chasing me would catch me.

Big mistake!

My delusions came to light when at mile 17 my legs cramped up. I was hobbling at this point, and at mile 20, the entire group caught me. As the group passed, I was left all alone in an open plain, resembling African grasslands. I was a wounded animal unaware of a lion peering through the grass ready to pounce on me. It was eerie, but in all honesty, I welcomed the feeling. I was in so much pain, and I wasn't even halfway done. The sun was beaming and I had run out of water. I walked gingerly along, careful not to trip on the limestone caps on the ground. I was not prepared and it showed. When running ultramarathons you can't make a lucky 3-pointer like in basketball. Either you prepared or you didn't.

The memory brings to mind a brilliant quote by Greek lyric poet and author, Archilochus that says, "You don't rise to the level of your expectations but fall to the level of your training." My expectations in the first 15 miles were that I might win the race. My training said, "You are lucky you lasted 15 miles, let alone finish 50 miles."

That's right! I finished!

I barely completed that 50-miler, but I did it. Everything hurt. I almost called it quits multiple times, but in the end, I made it. I was a new man. I had broken the pattern of waiting for the perfect time.

Now what?

Initially, I didn't have a vision, purpose or a long-term process for running and competing. For the past several years, prior to the race, I had teetered back and forth with my running. When I decided to focus on running daily it shifted my mindset and my habits. Now, running daily has allowed me to gain more clarity around my vision. I want to run and explore the most grueling adventures. Here are three bucket-list adventures that I want to prepare for:

1.) Run across the United States connecting the major trail systems.
2.) Run the Western States 100-Miler.

3.) Run the Grand Canyon South Rim to the North Rim and back to the South Rim in a day.

My purpose or what drives me to perform or train for these and other adventures is that these activities help me to become a better version of myself because they are tied into the process of improving. To endure these physically and mentally-demanding adventures, I need to train consistently. To become a man who trains consistently and is willing to get uncomfortable, I must become a man who is focused and diligent, a man who focuses on consistency and progress. I must become the type of man who is disciplined and meticulous.

In life, there are plenty of people who talk a good game and start strong. But it's the people who have that long-term view, who are the ones putting in the work daily who have the staying power.

If you want to build your powerful and purposeful legacy, first, create a crystal-clear vision, use your purpose to drive you and execute your process daily. Sharply define the steps you can take consistently throughout your life to live your legacy right now. Focus on taking one step at a time.

Be clear on the man you want to become and start living your life like that man today.

How do you want your kids to remember you? Start living that today. Perhaps you'd like to take your kids on extravagant, amazing vacations. Don't wait! Take them on that unforgettable vacation if you can. If you can't take them on that extravagant getaway right now, you can read to them for 30 minutes to an hour. You can spend time playing with them and talking with them. You can step into their world and interact with them. You can look at their interests, and make them your interests, or at least, you can acknowledge them, and figure out how to best connect with them. Think of the people who matter most in your life: how can you better connect with them right now? Don't wait until everything is perfect.

This book was designed to help you create clarity around the legacy you want to live and leave. Take a moment and reflect on these questions.

1.) What's one of the biggest takeaways you've gotten from reading this book that you can use to improve your life or the lives of others?

2.) How do you feel this book has helped you move closer to understanding and creating a legacy that excites and inspires you?

3.) What's one action you can take today to ensure you are moving one step closer to creating that legacy?

We don't have a say in our birth and don't know when our death is coming, but life and the impact we leave is comprised of the dash in between. If you want to live that dash and live your life to the fullest then do these three things:

- Get crystal clear on your vision.

- Uncover the purpose that drives you.

- Create a process that is simple, consistent, and precise.

Execute daily on your vision, purpose, and process and keep it in alignment with your values.

In each moment of each day, the life you live is the legacy you will leave.

Get **FREE** access to a special course that will walk you through the legacy creation process. I created this course just for you since you are reading this book.

Visit www.LegacyCodeBook.com/yourlegacy

GRATITUDE

First, I'd like to thank my amazing wife, Christian. You believe in me even when I am not certain. You support me when times are tough. You inspire me daily with your strength, focus, and love. You make living out my dreams a reality. Without you I wouldn't have been able to clearly communicate the message in this book. I love you always. I love that you were able to contribute to making this book flow and communicate what I wanted to say more effectively.

To Mandy, Amelie, and Aiden, thank you for loving me and sharing the simple joys in life. Thank you for your patience during the days and nights this book took me away from you.

To Mom, Thank you for your continual love and support. You amaze me with your actions and consistency of strength, sacrifice, and perseverance. Thank you for sowing the seeds of faith.

To Kika, you really helped me move forward with this book. Your constant push to finish it helped me keep going when it was easier to stop. Love you.

To Kara and Javo, thanks for believing in me and supporting me with your posts, comments, and questions.

To my amazing Tia Tere, who cheered and cried as you transcribed this book. You allowed me to get honest and vulnerable and brought it to life on paper. I love you.

To Mel, thank you for all your help transcribing and believing in me and my message. You are so worthy.

To my family, who cheered me on and believed I had something worth sharing.

To my Facebook friends and community who constantly challenged, celebrated, and supported me on this journey.

To Hilary, who believed in my vision and helped me, format, edit, and publish this book for all to read.

To Dax, your friendship and coaching literally transformed my life. Without you and Guru, this would not have been possible. I cherish you always buddy.

To Trevor, thank you for no longer allowing me to give excuses. You pushed me over the edge. I had been saying that I wanted to write a book for quite some time and now here it is.

To Brandon, your weekly support and coaching were instrumental in making the writing process and book itself come to life in a way that was congruent with me.

To the 111 men, I interviewed for this book and to my amazing clients who shared their intimate stories, insightful perspective, and tremendous support. Thank you for making this book rich and enlightening.

ABOUT THE AUTHOR

Armando Cruz is a connoisseur of experiences, husband, father, adventurer, best selling author, ultra-marathoner, lifestyle physical therapist, and legacy coach.

Armando helps growth-minded, married men live happier, more connected, and more fulfilled lives through his immersive coaching program that guides them to show up powerfully in their marriage, in their health, in their business, and in creating their purposeful legacy. Armando's unique approach helps strip away the clutter both internally and externally that stops men from showing up daily as the greatest and grandest version of who they are for themselves, their family, and their legacy.

He is the creator of the Cleanse & Renewal Program, the Modern Man Virtual Summit, and the R.I.C.H. Man Experience. He is the co-owner of Cruz Country Fitness & Physical Therapy with his wife, Christian.

Armando has climbed mountains, run over 50 miles in a day in swamps filled with snakes and alligators, has lived out of his car, and has rollerbladed and surfed in hurricanes but his biggest adventure has been fatherhood.

He is the proud dad of three amazing children and has been married for over 11, years to his beautiful wife, Christian.